Get Your Crochet On!
HIP HATS & COOL CAPS

Get Your Crochet On!

HIP HATS & COOL CAPS

Afya Ibomu

Photography by Shannon McCollum
and Shannon Washington

The Taunton Press

The Taunton Press
Inspiration for hands-on living®

Text © 2006 by Oudane Foster
Photos by Shannon McCollum: 2, 7–12, 16–19, 22–24, 28, 29, 32, 36, 39, 48–51,
56–59, 61, 66–70, 76–79, 84–91, 96–99, 104–106, 108–111, 116–119; Photos by Shannon Washington: 3–6, 13, 30, 33–35,
40, 44–47, 52, 54, 55, 62–65, 71–75, 80–83, 92–95, 100–103, 112–115; Photo by bossupbu.com: p. 122
Illustrations by Marcus Williams

The Taunton Press, Inc., 63 South Main Street, PO Box 5506, Newtown, CT 06470-5506
e-mail: tp@taunton.com

Editor: Pam Hoenig
Jacket/Cover and interior design: Shannon Washington
Layout: Shannon Washington and Cathy Cassidy
Illustrator: Marcus Williams
Photographers: Shannon McCollum and Shannon Washington
Cover Photographers: (front cover) left, Shannon Washington; right top and bottom, Shannon McCollum;
(back cover) left, bossupbu.com; right top, Shannon Washington; right bottom, Shanon McCollum

Library of Congress Cataloging-in-Publication Data

Ibomu, Afya.
  Get your crochet on! : hip hats & cool caps / Afya Ibomu ; photographers: Shannon McCollum and Shannon Washington.
     p. cm.
  Includes index.
  ISBN-13: 978-1-56158-850-3
  ISBN-10: 1-56158-850-4
  1. Crocheting. 2. Hats. I. Title.
  TT825.I23 2006
  746.43'40432--dc22
                                        2006011179

Printed in China
10 9 8 7 6 5 4 3 2 1

The following manufacturers/names appearing in Get Your Crochet On! are trademarks: Bernat®, Hobby Lobby℠,
Jo-Ann Fabric & Crafts℠, Lion Brand Yarns®, Michaels℠, Patons®, Red Heart®, Reynolds®, Wal-Mart℠

Acknowledgments

There were so many people involved in completing this book.

Mom, thanks for always having my back—you are my number-one fan. Thank you for helping me to greatly improve my crocheting skills and for helping to edit the book.

To Khnum, my love, my best friend, thanks for all of the brainstorming sessions, advice, support, and inspiration to boss up by any means necessary!

To my son, Itwela, thank you for all of your hugs, love, patience, and understanding while I was working long hours. I love you.

To Regina Brooks, my agent: You have really helped guide me through the publishing process. Thanks for your professionalism and hard work.

To earthmotherpress.com and Shaam Jones for helping me write the proposal that became this book, to Gwendolyn Faye and J. Carolyn Sanders for editing the patterns, to Marcus Williams for his illustrations, and to Shannon Washington for her interior and cover design.

To Shannon McCollum and Shannon Washington for the photography, to Kasema Kalifah for her fashion styling on location, and to the models: Erykah Badu, Darryl Brodie, Common, Jamila Crawford, Itwela Ibomu, Anishika Jontae, Khepera, M1, Azure Macklin, Sigele Messiah, Fanny Naritama, Roots, Umi, and Candice Vilaire.

I want to thank everyone who has bought my hats and designs over the years.

I give thanks to the ancestors, my family, and my friends for all of their love and support.

Ase'

Contents

The Patterns

Introduction

Get Your Crochet On! Hip Hats & Cool Caps is a trendsetting crochet artist's dream. The patterns featured in this book are as functional as they are fashionable. Whether cleverly concealing a "bad hair day" or boldly making a fashion statement, crocheted caps are appropriate for all seasons. These caps are extensions of their creator's and wearer's personality. With easy-to-follow instructions and encouraging photos, *Get Your Crochet On!* makes this timeless tradition accessible to crocheters of varied skill levels.

I wrote this book to capture and express the fresh and innovative styles of a funky, creative new generation of crochet artists and fans. My own personal style is a mix of street, hip-hop, '70s vintage, and new millennium.

Needle crafting runs in my family. I have aunts and cousins who crochet, knit, sew, do needlepoint, and quilt, and I guess you could say that my own journey with crochet began in the womb. My mom crocheted the entire time she was pregnant with me, but as soon as I was born, she put her hook and yarn down and did not pick them up for 22 years. My grandmother was a wonderful seamstress. She made elaborate, detailed wedding dresses and all the dresses for wedding parties. I grew up going to the fabric store with her to pick out my own material and patterns, usually something from the McCall's New York section.

It wasn't until my early 20s, though, that I finally learned to crochet. I was working as a merchandiser at one of the busiest retail stores in New York City, where I had started as a sales associate and worked my way up to head merchandiser. I really learned a lot about coordinating colors, fashion, and accessorizing.

One day I was sitting in the lunchroom, where a woman was crocheting. I asked her if she would show me what she was doing, and she did. I caught on fast. I started off making bags. They were simple—basically two rectangles joined together. Ironically, I had the hardest time trying to make a hat. But as soon as I got the basics down, my hats began to sell, and I started a custom hatmaking business called Who The Cap Fits. I now sell my hats at international festivals, at boutiques on the East Coast, and to celebrities. I have made many items for people like Common, Erykah Badu, Dead Prez, Talib Kweli, and Musiq (Soulchild), and my hats have been seen in music videos, on album covers, and in fashion magazines.

One of the great things about crochet is that it is a very inexpensive craft. All you need is a skein of yarn and a hook. Many of the patterns in this book can be made for $12 or less.

In *Get Your Crochet On!* you will find:

- The basics of crochet: stitches, techniques, and tools
- The freedom to express your own style through 20 original patterns
- Hip designs that add flair and pizzazz to your wardrobe
- Priceless, one-of-a-kind gift ideas

- Hours of crochet fun
- A renewed motivation and appreciation for the art of crochet

Crochet transfers your energy and brings it to life through a hook and yarn. Using your two hands, you have the ability to create memories that become a part of people's lives. So grab a skein and a hook and *Get Your Crochet On!*

Getting Started!

What You Need

The tools needed to crochet are few and basic—really, just a hook and some yarn. A couple of other items will allow you to give your projects a finished look.

Yarn

At some point in my crocheting life, I became a yarn fiend. I shop for yarn all over the country—at flea markets, in craft and yarn stores—but my favorite place to find yarn is thrift stores. Thrift stores have very inexpensive yarn. You can find unique, old-school yarn with distinctive colors that are no longer made. Color is such an important part of the art of crochet. The use of one subtle hue can transform a hat and make it totally unique. It's fun to be creative with your color choices and use your environment for inspiration.

All of my patterns can be made using sport- or worsted-weight cotton or acrylic yarns. Worsted yarns are medium-weight yarns, and the most common kind. Sport-weight yarns are a little thinner, or lighter, than worsted-weight yarns.

Acrylic yarns are synthetic, but have a bulky feel similar to wool. For fall and winter, you will want to use sport, worsted, or chunky acrylic yarns (which are thicker yet than worsted) for the warmth. Acrylic yarns are also good for making an item stiff, like a bib. They come in a very large selection of colors and are generally very affordable.

Cotton yarn, a natural fiber, is softer than acrylic, and comes in sport and worsted weight as well. In spring and summer, use cotton to keep your head cool. You can mix in a sport-weight acrylic for an accent, like I did in Talkin' Blues on page 62.

I use nylon yarn to give my hats a dressier look. Nylon has a glossy sheen that is similar to some types of cotton yarn. Nylon yarn gives your work a fancier look than acrylic yarn does, and it's as sturdy as acrylic without being as bulky. Nylon comes in two different thicknesses that are comparable to sport- and worsted-weight acrylic. Textured novelty yarns—which

Sport-weight cotton

Sport-weight acrylic

Worsted-weight acrylic

Chunky yarn

Textured yarn

Nylon yarn

are made from a wide variety of synthetic and natural fibers—are great for adding flair to any hat and come in many different weights and textures. Unfortunately, they are usually very expensive.

Crocheting with double strands

In some of my patterns, I'll instruct you to crochet with two strands of yarn at once (the same yarn or two different yarns) for one of several reasons. First, the resulting crocheted fabric is stiffer than it would be if you used just one strand, and this gives extra body to certain features, such as the bib of a hat. Second, crocheting with two strands of yarn in different weights or colors will give you a unique color or texture effect. And finally, combining yarns allows you to mix different weights of yarn in the same hat, yet get an even result. For example, if the hat you're making is predominantly crocheted in worsted-weight yarn, but you want to use a particular sport-weight yarn for a section of it, crochet that portion with a double strand of sport weight to get the same approximate weight as the worsted. Do the same thing if you are crocheting with a chunky yarn but want to use a certain worsted yarn for part of it. Or, you can use a double strand for a whole cap if the pattern asks for a heavier weight yarn and your yarn of choice is lighter in weight.

Each skein of yarn has two ends. One is on the outside of the skein, the other is located in the middle of the skein. It's preferable to use the end in the center, but you may have to dig into the middle through both ends of the skein to find it. To crochet with double strands, grab both the outside and center ends, hold them together as one strand, and start crocheting.

Hooks

The hook has a few distinct parts on it. The tip is inserted into the previously made stitch. The throat hooks the yarn and pulls it through the stitch. The shaft holds the loops you're working with, and its thickness determines the size of your stitch. The thumb rest allows you to rotate the hook easily as you make each stitch. The handle is used for balance and leverage to help keep your hook steady and for maneuvering your hook properly.

Everyone has a favorite type of hook to use, and if you're a beginner, it won't be long until you do, too. Each kind of hook has a different weight and feel in your hand, and some work better than others with particular kinds of yarn. The right hook is the one that feels best in your hand and works most effectively with the yarn you're using.

Plastic hooks are usually recommended for beginning crocheters. Lightweight and inexpensive, they work well with lighter yarns like sport weight. Personally, they feel a little flimsy to me, and I've even broken a few when crocheting with double strands.

Aluminum hooks are very sturdy, reasonably priced, and one of the best types of hook to use when crocheting with double strands or chunky yarns. They also seem to make your stitch a slight bit tighter.

Wood and bamboo hooks are my personal favorites because of the way they feel in my hand. They're wonderful for working with sport- and worsted-weight yarns, but sometimes they are not sturdy enough for work with double strands.

Bone hooks feel great, but sometimes the tips are not very smooth, can catch on the yarn, and can cause fraying. They work better with lighter-weight yarns, like sport-weight cotton.

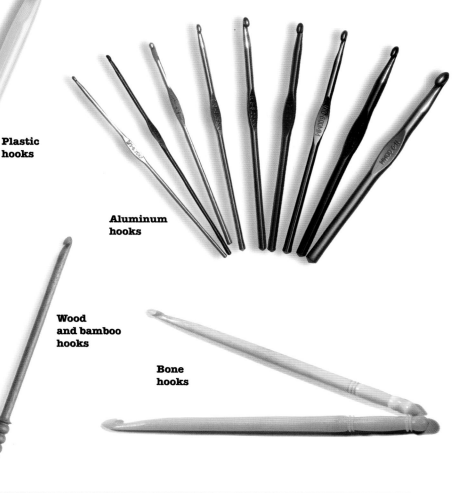

Plastic hooks

Aluminum hooks

Wood and bamboo hooks

Bone hooks

Hook sizes

The size of a crochet hook is based on its thickness, and it also corresponds to the weight of the yarn you're using. Lighter-weight yarns, like sport weight, require smaller-sized hooks, and thicker yarns, like chunky or doubled yarns, will require larger hooks.

    Hooks are measured by two different sizing systems. The American system is based on letters and numbers. The higher the number or the further along the letter of the alphabet, the larger the hook. In the second system, based on the metric system and used in Europe and Canada, the hook width is measured in millimeters—the bigger the number, the thicker the hook. All the patterns in this book were crocheted with American hooks, but in the instructions, I will give the suggested hook sizes in both American and metric figures, so you're covered no matter what's available in your area. And even if you're using the recommended size hook for a given project, always remember to check your gauge before starting and adjust your hook size if necessary (see page 25 for more on this).

Crochet Hook Size Equivalents

American	Metric (mm)
B/1	2.25 mm
C/2	2.75 mm
D/3	3.25 mm
E/4	3.5 mm
F/5	3.75 mm
G/6	4.0 mm
H/8	5.0 mm
I/9	5.5 mm
J/10	6.0 mm
K/10	6.5 mm
N	9.0 mm
P	10.0 mm
Q	15.0 mm

Additional Tools

Finally, you'll want some basic sewing tools on hand for finishing your hats. Scissors are needed to cut loose threads. A selection of embroidery and weaving needles comes in handy for weaving in yarn ends and adding elastic for a snug fit. Sewing needles and thread will help secure snaps on cap visors or bibs. A tape measure is necessary for checking your gauge and measuring your work as you crochet, and fabric glue can be used to secure yarn ends firmly and prevent unraveling.

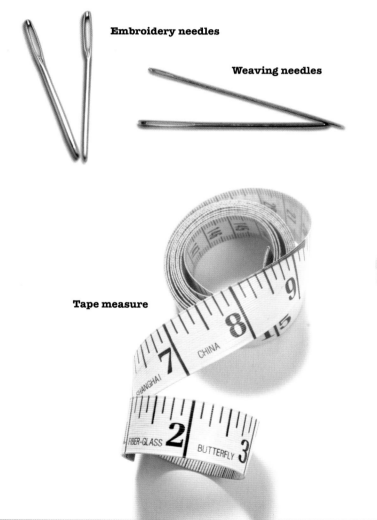

Embroidery needles

Weaving needles

Tape measure

½-inch elastic

Snaps

Round elastic

Glue

Aleene's® STOP FRAYING®

PREVENTS FABRICS & TRIMS FROM FRAYING & UNRAVELING

4 FL OZ (118 mL)

Thread

Colors, Colors, Colors

Choosing colors can be as simple as picking your favorite color or trying to match an outfit. I have always been inspired by nature and the world around me. Each season has its own color scheme with its own energy. Here are a few colors that correspond to each season.

- **Spring:** Pastels, like pink and light greens, blues and yellows
- **Summer:** Red, orange, yellow, turquoise, blue, bright green and sand
- **Autumn:** Amber, orange, brown, and green
- **Winter:** Gray, winter white, black, and blue

Spring

Summer

Autumn

Winter

The Color Wheel and Basic Color Theory

Using a color wheel will help you choose a pleasing mix of colors as well as open your mind to color combinations that you may not have thought of using. Please refer to and use the color wheel on the next page to help you with your selections.

The primary colors are yellow, red, and blue. These are the colors that cannot be made by mixing other colors.

Secondary colors are those made by combining primary colors. They are:

- Red + blue = violet (purple)
- Blue + yellow = green
- Yellow + red = orange

Tertiary colors are a mix of a primary color and one of the secondary colors next to it on the color wheel. The six tertiary colors are:

- Blue + green = turquoise
- Green + yellow = lime green
- Violet + red = crimson
- Red + orange = red-orange
- Yellow + orange = yellow-orange
- Blue + violet = blue-violet

Primary colors

Secondary colors

Tertiary colors

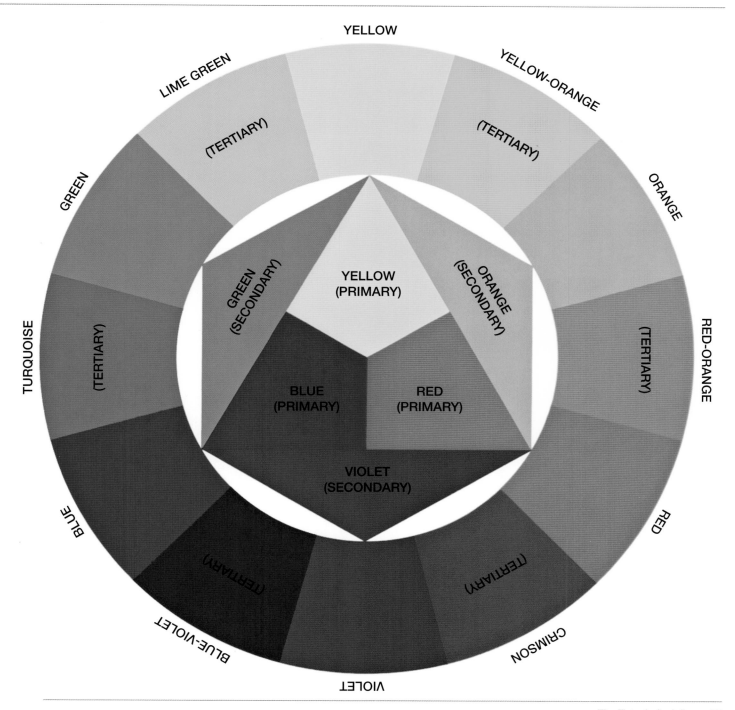

The Basics

In this section, I'm going to cover everything you need to know to be able to crochet these hats, even if you've never picked up a crochet hook before today. Among other things, you'll learn how to hold a crochet hook, how to make all the stitches called for in the patterns, and some other useful techniques.

Making a Slip Knot

Every crocheted project begins with a slip knot. After you make it, slip it onto your hook.

1. Loop the yarn around your index finger and grab the yarn with your thumb and middle finger.

3. Pull the end of the yarn through the loop.

2. Bring the yarn behind and around the loop.

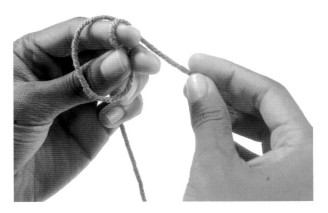

4. Pull the yarn gently.

Holding Your Crochet Hook

There are two ways you can hold the hook, and which you choose is simply a matter of your own personal comfort.

You can hold the hook like a pencil • • •

• • • **or** you can hold it like a knife.

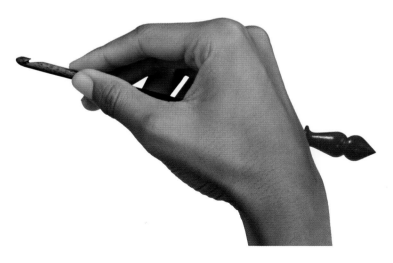

Crochet Abbreviations

All crochet patterns use abbreviations in their directions. Here are the ones you'll come across in this book.

ch	chain
cl	cluster
dc	double crochet
ea	each
hdc	half double crochet
oz	ounces
pff st	puff stitch
rnd	round
sc	single crochet
sk	skip
sl	slip
sp(s)	space(s)
st, sts	stitch(es)
tr	triple or treble crochet
yo	yarn over
*	asterisk is used to mark the beginning of a part of the instructions that will be worked more than once

Holding the Yarn

First, make a slip knot and place it on your hook. Hold the hook in your dominant hand.

1. With your fingers spread, drape the yarn over the last three fingers and behind the pointer finger of your other hand.

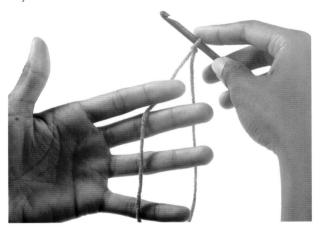

2. Bring the yarn over your pointer finger and hold it between your thumb and middle finger.

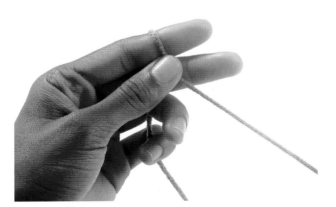

As you crochet, you need to secure the yarn in your hand to add some tension or you'll be crocheting very loosely. You can either:

Hold the yarn that leads to the skein loosely with your pinkie and ring finger • • •

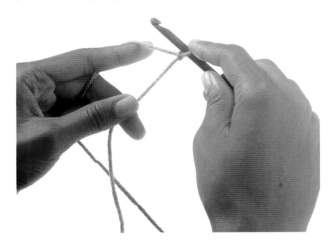

• • • or wrap the yarn around your pinkie (do whichever feels best).

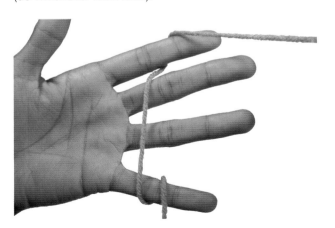

Yarn Over (yo)

The yarn over is the most basic technique in crocheting. It is a component of every crochet stitch. To yarn over, wrap the yarn over your hook from back to front (clockwise), then proceed as directed by your pattern.

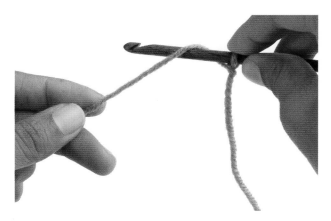

Chain Stitch (ch)

Make a slip knot and place it on your hook. Grab the yarn with the hook (moving the hook around the yarn clockwise) and pull it through the slip knot.

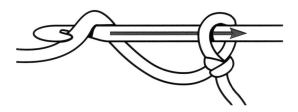

Counting chain stitches

Always start with the first chain away from the hook and count toward the start of the chain. Do not count the slip knot or the loop presently on the hook as part of the chain.

Slip Stitch (sl st)

Insert your hook into a stitch or space as directed, yarn over, and pull the yarn through the stitch and the loop on the hook.

Single Crochet (sc)

Insert your hook into a stitch or space as directed, yarn over (figure 1), and pull the yarn through the stitch; you now have two loops on the hook. Yarn over and pull yarn through both loops (figure 2).

Figure 1

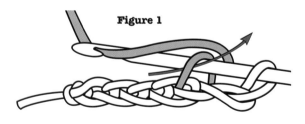

Figure 2

Half Double Crochet (hdc)

Yarn over, insert the hook into a stitch or space as directed, yarn over (figure 3), and pull yarn through the stitch; you now have three loops on the hook. Yarn over and pull yarn through all three loops on the hook (figure 4).

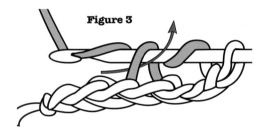

Figure 3

Figure 4

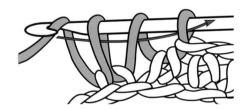

Double Crochet (dc)

Yarn over, insert the hook into a stitch or space as directed, yarn over, and pull yarn through the stitch; you now have three loops on the hook. Yarn over and pull yarn through the first two loops on the hook (figure 5); you now have two loops on the hook. Yarn over again and pull yarn through the last two loops on the hook (figure 6).

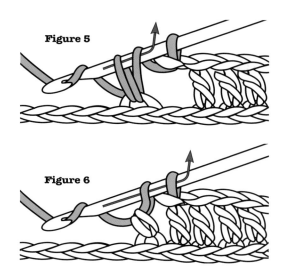

Figure 5

Figure 6

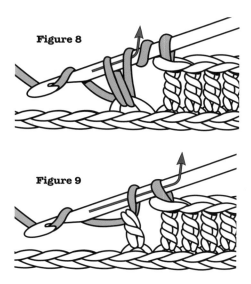

Figure 8

Figure 9

Triple (or Treble) Crochet (tr)

Yarn over two times, insert the hook into a stitch or space as directed, yarn over, and pull yarn through the stitch (figure 7); you now have four loops on the hook. Yarn over and pull yarn through the first two loops on the hook (figure 8); you now have three loops on the hook. Yarn over again and pull yarn through the next two loops on the hook; you now have two loops on the hook. Yarn over again and pull yarn through the last two loops on the hook (figure 9).

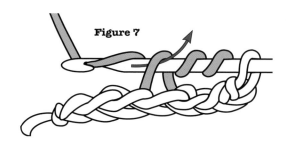

Figure 7

Puff Stitch (pff st)

Yarn over, insert the hook into a stitch or space, yarn over, and pull yarn through; you now have three loops on the hook. Yarn over, insert the hook in the same stitch, yarn over, and pull yarn through again. You now have five loops on the hook. Yarn over and pull yarn through all five loops.

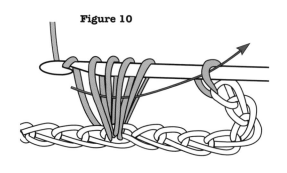

Figure 10

Working in Rows

All crochet projects start with a *chain.* Once you've gotten the proper number of stitches in your chain (see "Counting Chain Stitches" on page 19), you will crochet back into each of the chain stitches using whatever stitch your pattern calls for. Unless you're otherwise directed, to crochet into a stitch, you'll insert your hook under the top two threads of the stitch (see figure 10).

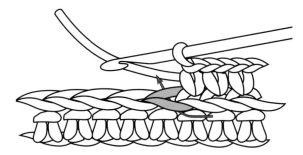

Figure 10

Before beginning the next row, you'll make one or more chain stitches (your pattern will tell you how many; for example, ch 1 means to make 1 chain stitch), then flip the piece over, or turn, so that you can work back across the row. The chain stitch or stitches at the end of a row are called the turning chain.

Which stitch to begin with on a new row

Your pattern will tell you which stitch on a row to begin with. For example, it might say, "Sc into 1st st from hook," meaning you'll work a single crochet into the first stitch away from your hook, or "Dc into 2nd st from hook," meaning you'll work a double crochet into the second stitch away from your hook. Follow the pattern directions to the end of the row, chain as directed, turn, and continue.

Working in first stitch from hook.

Working in second stitch from hook.

Working in Rounds

For a number of the hats in this book, you're going to be working in the round, making a crocheted circle that's going to turn into a hat. In several of the patterns, you'll also have to crochet in the round to close the top of the hat.

To make a ring, join chain by working a slip stitch into the first stitch of the chain.

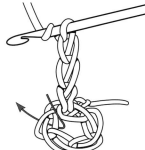

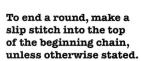

To begin the next round, chain as directed in your pattern, then crochet into the ring, not into the chain stitches.

To end a round, make a slip stitch into the top of the beginning chain, unless otherwise stated.

Begin a round like you begin a row: make a chain, but instead of crocheting back into the chain, you'll join one end of it to the other using a slip stitch to create a ring. Then, like working in rows, you work a chain for the first stitch, then crochet however many stitches are required into the center of the ring (not into the chain stitches themselves).

When you get to the end of the round, join the end of the round with the beginning of it before going on to

the next round. Do this by making a slip stitch into the top of the first stitch of the round. To work the next row, you'll be instructed to chain, then work into the stitches and/or spaces.

Which stitch to begin with in a new round

As with working in rows, you may be instructed to start each round in a specific stitch (for example, the first or second stitch from the hook). If no stitch is specified, assume you'll begin in the first stitch.

Working into the first stitch from the hook.

Working in second stitch from hook.

Working into the Front or Back of a Stitch

In several of the patterns, you will be asked to work into the front or the back loop of a stitch instead of picking up both threads. This technique creates a raised, textured look that I like.

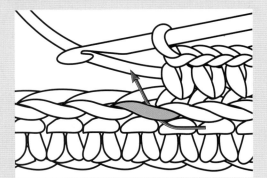

Crocheting into the front loop of a stitch.

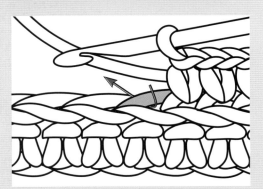

Crocheting into the back loop of a stitch.

Count your stitches

It's very important that you check your stitch count at the end of every row to make sure you haven't skipped or added any stitches. If you don't count for a couple of rows or rounds and find out you've got the wrong number of stitches, it's going to be difficult to figure out where you made the mistake.

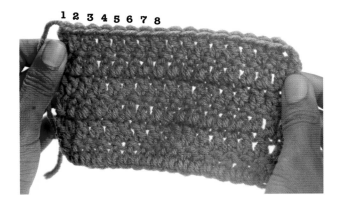

Counting stitches in a row.

Counting stitches in a round.

Getting Your Gauge

For many years, I did not even think about gauge. It seemed confusing and time-consuming. I just made something and hoped it would come out right. After I made many adult hats that came out small enough for a baby, I realized that getting the right gauge before you begin your project actually saves you time and frustration.

Gauge is used to determine the finished size of your project. It is the number of stitches and the number of rows or rounds in 1 square inch of crocheted fabric. Every crochet pattern you'll run across is based on a particular gauge, and that information is usually found at the top of a pattern. It may look something like this: 14 sts = 4". In addition, every skein of yarn you buy will have its recommended gauge listed on its label.

Why not just match the gauge on the pattern with the gauge on a yarn label?

That would seem to make sense, but the truth is that everyone crochets differently, even when using the same yarn and the same hook. For instance, my mother crochets much tighter than I do. The weather, your state of mind, or even your experience working with a particular type of yarn can also affect your gauge. That's why it's always a good idea to crochet a gauge swatch before you start your project.

To do this, with the yarn you intend to use and the size of hook suggested in your pattern, crochet a swatch using the project's stitch pattern that is at least 4 inches long and 4 inches wide. At that point, use a tape measure or knitter's window to measure your stitch gauge (how many stitches you are getting per

4 inches measuring across a row) and your row gauge (how many rows you are getting per 4 inches measuring up and down). If you're getting more stitches or rows than is called for, switch to a hook one size up, crochet another swatch, and check your gauge again. Keep moving up a size until you get the gauge you're looking for. If you are getting fewer stitches or rows than is called for, switch to a hook one size smaller and check again.

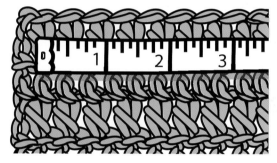

Measuring gauge with a tape measure.

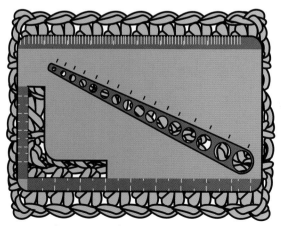

Measuring gauge with a knitter's window.

Joining New Yarn

In some of my patterns (when adding a bib to a hat, for example), you have to begin crocheting mid-row or in some other specified spot (like "join at any seam").

To join yarn to crocheted work, insert your hook into the work as instructed in the pattern and pull up a loop of the new yarn, leaving a short tail for weaving in later on (figure 11). Work one chain, then continue to follow the directions.

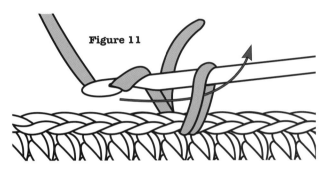

Figure 11

Changing Colors

When changing colors, don't finish the last stitch using the old color; leave two loops on the hook. Grab the new color with the hook (figure 12) and pull it through both loops to complete the stitch (figure 13). Continue working with the new color.

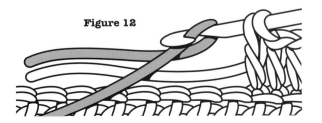

Figure 12

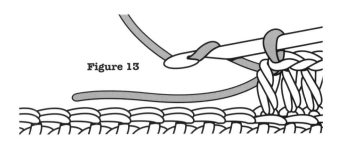

Figure 13

Fastening Off

When you are finished with a piece, clip the yarn about 5 inches away from the hook, then pull the thread through the last stitch (figure 14).

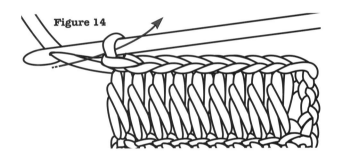

Figure 14

Finishing Touches

Once you've completed all or most all of your crocheting, you're in the home stretch. Here, we'll cover putting the pieces together, finishing techniques, and some fun add-ons you can use to customize your crowns.

Joining Seams

Some of my hats are created by crocheting separate panels, then joining them, either by sewing or crocheting them together. Usually, you will want to use the same color of yarn that was used in the pattern to do this, but you can also use a different color to add a little flavor, like a gold seam on a pair of jeans. Most seams will show up on the wrong side (the inside) of the hat, making the edges invisible, but in a few, like Talkin' Blues, the seams are on the outside for a different effect.

As you join the panels, make sure the stitches along each edge match up. If you're crocheting pieces together, use the same size hook that was used in the pattern, unless otherwise stated.

Backstitch seam

Hold the sides of the panels together with the right or wrong sides facing each other, depending on the effect you want for the hat. Using a weaving needle, work a backstitch seam along the edge.

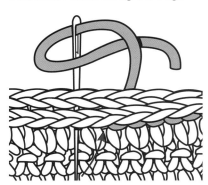

Joining two pieces with a backstitch seam

Slip-stitch seam

Hold the sides of the panels together with the right or wrong sides facing each other, depending on the effect you want for the hat. Work a row of slip stitch, going through both loops of each stitch on each piece. You can also join them together by crocheting through the back or front loops of each stitch. This will create a flatter seam.

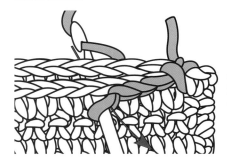

Joining two pieces using slip stitch

Single-crochet seam

Hold the sides of the panels together with the right or wrong sides facing each other, depending on the effect you want for the hat. Work a row of single crochet, going through both loops of each stitch on each piece.

Joining two pieces with single crochet

Weaving in Yarn Ends

For a long time, when I finished a crocheted piece, I would just tie a knot in my yarn ends and call it a day. But my mother taught me how to weave in yarn ends, saying, "Presentation is half the sale." It really does make a difference—your hat will look more finished, and weaving in ends will keep your work from coming apart. Securing the end of the yarn with fabric glue after you weave it in is optional. I started using fabric glue when I found that, after a few washes, the woven-in ends would start to peek out the front of the hat, or the garment would begin to unravel. Adding a small dab of glue to the cut yarn ends after weaving them really keeps them in place. Some of my customers have been wearing their hats for six or seven years, and the ends are still secure.

Now You See It, Now You Don't

When the wrong sides of the panels are facing each other, the seam will be on the outside (the right side) of the piece. When the right sides are facing each other, the seam will appear on the inside (the wrong side) of the piece.

1. Using a weaving needle, weave the yarn through like-colored stitches on the wrong side of the hat. Try to weave it through at least four stitches.

2. Cut the yarn close to the last stitch.

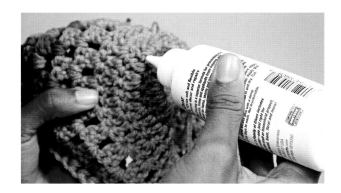

3. Glue the tip of the yarn down, using just a little bit of glue (this step is optional).

Weaving in and Covering Elastic

I used to get frustrated after wearing one of my hats a couple of times, when I'd find that it just didn't fit me the way it did when I first put it on. I began experimenting with using different types of elastic to keep my hats snug, as well as finding different ways to cover the elastic up. A friend of mine, an extremely talented seamstress and needlecraft artist named Kephera Ife, came up with the idea of crocheting over the elastic to hide it.

For the majority of the patterns in this book, you can use round cord elastic and a weaving needle. For the O.G. pattern, you can use ½-inch-thick elastic and weave it through the hat using a safety pin.

1. Weave the elastic through the last row of crochet, making sure not to pull it too tight. You don't want the hat to pucker. When you've woven the elastic all the way through, you can adjust it by pulling it a bit tighter.

2. Tie a knot in the elastic and put a tiny bit of glue on the knot.

To cover the elastic, using a size H/8 hook and 2 strands of yarn, join the yarn in the last stitch you worked with the right side facing you. Ch 1, go through next st, *[yo, pull through (2 loops on hook), yo, go through next st, yo, pull through (4 loops on hook), yo, pull through all 4 loops, yo, go through same st]*. Repeat from * all the way around the hat, then join with sl st.

Edging

When you want to join a panel, make a border, or smooth out an edge, you often have to work into what are called *row-end stitches*. Row-end stitches are worked into the side of a stitch rather than the stitch itself and appear, as you might expect, at the ends of rows.

For example, if you are working in rows and you want to add a border around your piece of work, you would turn your work on its side, chain the indicated number of stitches, then insert your hook into the side of the stitch and crochet around the piece.

When working across row-end stitches, insert the hook where two stitches join together, at the base or the top of the stitches, or both. You want to avoid gaps or holes across the edges. If the edge of your crocheted piece has end posts of double or triple crochet, you will have to work more than one stitch into each row-end stitch. If you are putting an edge on more than one panel or piece of the same size, try to end up with the same number of edging stitches on each one.

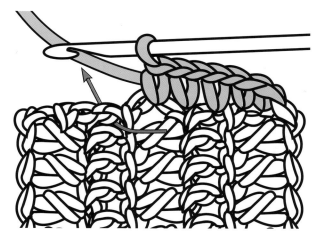

Single-crochet edging worked into row-end stitches

Making a Bib

A bib (also called a bill, like the kind on a baseball cap) is a wonderful addition to many of the hats in this book. It adds a simple, stylish flair and only takes a few extra minutes to crochet. There's one thing to keep in mind when adding a bib: Don't join the yarn where you joined the last round. If you do, you'll end up with a visible seam.

Smaller bib

Use a size G/6 hook and 2 strands of the yarn you worked the hat in. Join yarn at edge of hat.

Row 1: Ch 1 (count as 1st st now and throughout), 1 sc in next st, *(2 sc in next st, 1 sc in next 2 sts). Repeat from * until there are 22 sts total.

Row 2: Ch 1, turn, (in back loops only on this row) 1 sc in 2nd st and in each st to end of row, 1 hdc in last row of hat, 1 sl st in next 2 sts. (26 sts)

Row 3: Ch 1, turn, 1 sc in 2nd st and in each st to end, 1 hdc in last row of hat, 1 sl st in next 2 sts. (29 sts)

Row 4: Ch 1, turn, 1 sc in 2nd st, *(1 sc in next 3 sts, 2 sc in next st), rep from * to end, 1 hdc in last row of hat, 1 sl st in next 2 sts. (39 sts)

Row 5: Repeat Row 3. (43 sts)
        Fasten off.

To get the curve you want in your bib, at the end of each row, work a half double crochet into the last row of the hat (see arrow), then make slip stitches into the next two stitches.

Larger bib

Use a size G/6 hook and 2 strands of the yarn you worked the hat in. Join yarn at edge of hat.

Row 1: Ch 1 (count as first st now and throughout). 1 sc in next st, *(2 sc in next st, 1 sc in next 2 sts). Repeat from * until there are 22 sts total.

Row 2: Ch 1, turn, (in back loops only on this row) 1 sc in 2nd st from hook, 1 sc in each st to end of row, 1 hdc in last row of hat, 1 sl st in next 2 sts. (26 sts)

Row 3: Ch 1, turn. 1 sc in 2nd st from hook, *(1 sc in next 3 sts, 2 sc in next st). Repeat from * to end, 1 hdc in last row of hat, 1 sl st in next 2 sts. (33 sts)

Row 4: Ch 1, turn. 1 sc in 2nd st from hook, 1 sc in each st to end of row, 1 hdc in last row, 1 sl st in next 2 sts. (36 sts)

Row 5: Ch 1, turn. 1 sc in 2nd st from hook, 1 sc in next 4 sts, *(2 sc in next st, 1 sc in next 5 sts). Repeat from * to end, 1 hdc in last row of hat, 1 sl st in next 2 sts. (44 sts)

Row 6: Repeat Row 4. (45 sts)
        Fasten off.

Lively Up (p. 100) with earflaps amd without the bib

Making Earflaps

General instructions for earflaps are given here, but they can be as large or as long as you want, and you can make them the same color as your hat or a different color to add unique flavor.

Use a size H/8 (5 mm) hook and 2 strands of the yarn you worked the hat in.

Ch 10 sts.

Row 1:	1 sc in 2nd st from hook (now and throughout) and each st to end of row. (9 sts)
Row 2:	Ch 1, turn, (in back loops only through Row 9) 1 sc in next 6 sts, 1 sl st in next 3 sts. (10 sts)
Row 3:	Ch 1, turn, 1 sl st in next 3 sts, 1 sc in each st to end of row. (10 sts)
Rows 4, 6, 8:	Repeat Row 2.
Rows 5, 7, 9:	Repeat Row 3.

Work a sc edging around flap and join.
Fasten off.

Repeat Rows 1–9 and edging for second earflap.
Fasten off

.

Adding ties

Join yarn on edge of small side of flap in the 4th st in from the end.

Row 1:   Ch 1, 1 sc in next 2 sts.

Row 2:   Ch 1, turn, 1 sc in next st.

Rows   Repeat Row 2.
3–25:

Joining earflaps to hat

Place flaps where you want them and join them with a sl st seam (see page 27), going through back loops only. Be sure they're positioned to cover your ears.

Making the ties

Work a single-crochet edging around each flap.

Join each flap to the hat using slip stitches.

Making Pom-Poms

Pom-poms add flair to your hat and can be made as big as you want.

Figure 15

1. Cut a piece of cardboard (if no size is specified in the pattern, cut it 1½ inches wide by 5 inches long). Cut a short slit in one end. Cut a 9-inch piece of yarn; lay it across the cardboard and secure one end in the slit. Wrap two strand of yarn (or however many strands you choose) around the cardboard 40 to 100 times, depending on the thickness you want (figure 15).

Figure 16

2. Tie the 9-inch piece of yarn around the wrapped yarn at the top of the cardboard, making a strong knot. Cut the wrapped yarn at the bottom of the cardboard (figures 16 and 17).

Figure 17

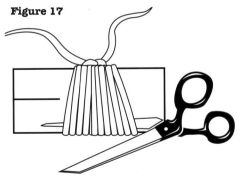

3. Remove the pom-pom from the cardboard. It may be necessary to wrap a 9-inch piece around the yarn again to tighten it some more. Trim the pom-pom to get a full, rounded shape (figure 18). Use the two long ends of the tie to secure the pom-pom to your hat. To tightly secure a pom-pom to your hat, weave the yarn ends through the hat, back through the pom-pom, then back into the hat.

Figure 18

Making Fringe

A fringe, in one or several colors, is a nice finishing touch. Using many strands of yarn can add a fuller look. To make your fringe, you'll cut lengths of yarn, fold them in half, and attach them to your hat. To figure out how long the lengths should be, decide how long you want your finished fringe to be. Multiply that number by 2, then add 2. For example, if you want the fringe to be 10 inches long, calculate the lengths you'll need to cut like this: 10 x 2 = 20 + 2 = 22 inches.

The 2 inches are added to compensate for a knot you'll be making and you double the final length because you have to fold the fringe in half.

1. Measure and cut the yarn into the necessary number of equal lengths. For example, if each fringe has 2 strands and you have 20 stitches across the edge you are attaching the fringe to, then you'll need 40 equal lengths of yarn.

2. Fold the number of strands needed for one fringe in half, making a loop at one end and matching the cut ends on the other.

3. Use your crochet hook to pull the loop through or around the stitch you are attaching the fringe to (figure 19).

4. Pull the loose ends of the yarn through the loop (figure 20).

5. Pull gently on the fringe ends to tighten the knot.

6. After you have added all the fringes, trim the ends so they are even.

Figure 19

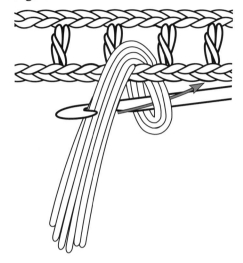

Figure 20

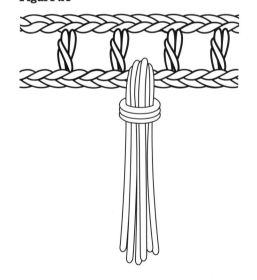

A Little TLC

Whether a hat needs to be hand washed or can be machine washed depends on the care instructions given on the yarn label, your resources, and whether the yarn has been preshrunk (some manufacturers will tell you that on the label, some won't). Before washing any piece, read the care instructions on the label (that means save the label!) and follow them. Most cotton yarns can safely be hand washed in cool to lukewarm water; most acrylic yarns can be machine washed and dried. Some yarn manufacturers will recommend dry cleaning to protect themselves, but often a garment made from the yarn really can be washed. The easiest way to tell for sure if a garment can be laundered is to make a swatch and test it (you could use your gauge swatch for this). Measure the swatch, then wash it, dry it, and remeasure it. This may sound like a lot of work, but I have learned from experience that this will save you a lot of headaches. After you have crocheted for a while and used different types of yarns, you will find a brand you like to work with and become familiar with its cleaning requirements.

To machine wash

Use cool to lukewarm water on a gentle or delicate cycle setting. Turn the hat inside out and place it in a mesh laundry bag, then wash it.

To hand wash

Place a gentle soap or detergent in a sink large enough to hold the hat. Add cool to lukewarm water and mix the soap into the water. Turn the hat inside out, place it in a mesh laundry bag, and set it in the water. Let it soak for about 20 minutes, swishing it around a couple of times. Drain the water and refill the sink with cool to lukewarm water to rinse. Place the hat in the water and gently swish it around a bit. Keep draining and refilling the sink until the water stays clear, then drain the sink. Let the hat drain thoroughly in the sink, then lightly press on it to release more water. To remove the remaining water, either put the hat in the washer on the spin cycle or roll it in a towel.

To dry

You may lay your hat on a flat surface, like a counter or the top of the washer or dryer, with a towel under it, or hang it on the side of the tub, or place it on a plastic or wood (not wire) hanger until it is dry. Hats made from cotton or acrylic yarn may be turned inside out and placed in the dryer on a low temperature setting for about 10 minutes just to remove excess water. After 10 minutes, remove it from the dryer and dry as recommended above.

Dry cleaning

I would recommend dry cleaning any hat made from a textured yarn. I've washed hats made out of such yarns only to have them turn into fuzz balls. Again, read the yarn label. When in doubt, dry-clean!

Getting rid of fuzzies

Use an old electric razor or a fuzz remover (these can usually be found in a drugstore or discount store) to shave the fuzz from a hat.

Universal Care Symbols

Here are some of the symbols that are likely to show up on your yarn labels. It's a good idea to keep one yarn label for every project you make, gluing a piece of the yarn to it, for future laundering reference.

 Hand wash

 Machine wash in lukewarm water

 Machine dry

 Do not machine dry

 Bleach

 Do not bleach

 Iron

 Do not iron

 Dry clean

 Do not dry clean

 Dry clean using "P" solvents

The Patterns!

Mellow Moods

This hat was inspired by the '70s cinema fashion.

Materials needed:

Size H/8 (5 mm) crochet hook, or size needed to obtain gauge

Round cord elastic

Weaving needle

Gauge:

12 dc = 4"

Directions

Using 2 strands of yarn, ch 16.

Row 1: 1 dc in 2nd ch from hook, 1 dc in each to end. (15 sts)

Row 2: Ch 2, turn, (in back loops only throughout) 1 dc in next 9 sts, 1 hdc in next 2 sts, 1 sc in next 2 sts, 1 sl st in last 2 sts. (15 sts)

Rnds 3: Ch 1, turn, 1 sl st in next 2 sts, 1 sc in next 2 sts, 1 hdc in next 2 sts, 1 dc in next 9 sts. (15 sts)

Row 4 and all even rows through Row 32: Repeat Row 2.

Row 5 and all odd rows through Row 31: Repeat Row 3.

Finishing

With wrong side facing out, join the first and last rows together with a slip-stitch seam (see page 27). Fasten off.

With right side facing out, join yarn at seam on wider opening of hat. Work a half double crochet edging all the way around. Don't fasten off.

Mellow Moods... continued

Adding elastic

Using a weaving needle, weave the elastic through the edging, then cover it, following the directions on page 29. Don't fasten off.

Making the brim

Continue to use the 2 strands of yarn.

Rnd 1: Ch 1, (in back loops only for this rnd) *(1 sc in next 5 sts, 2 sc in next st), repeat from * around, join.

Rnd 2: Ch 1, *(1 sc in next 6 sts, 2 sc in next st), repeat from * around, join.

Rnd 3: Ch 1, *(1 sc in next 7 sts, 2 sc in next st), repeat from * around, join.

Rnd 4: Ch 1, *(1 sc in next 8 sts, 2 sc in next st), repeat from * around, join.

Rnds 5–7: Ch 1, 1 sc in ea st around.

Rnd 8: Ch 1, *(1 sc in next 9 sts, 2 sc in next st), repeat from * around, join.

Rnd 9: Repeat Rnd 5. Fasten off.

Closing the top

With wrong side facing out, join a single strand of yarn at seam.

Rnd 1: Ch 1, 1 hdc in ea st around, join.

Rnd 2: Ch 1, *(sk next st, 1 hdc in next st), repeat from * around.

If necessary, repeat Row 2.
Close hole with sl st. Fasten off.

Bunny

This bun holder is a great way to put your hair up. It is wonderful on a hot day as well as a bad hair day.

Make your bunnies in a rainbow of solids or stripes.

Materials needed:

One 2 oz (60 g) skein of sport-weight yarn

Size G/6 (4 mm) crochet hook, or size needed to obtain gauge

For covering elastic, size H/8 (5 mm) crochet hook

Round cord elastic

Weaving needle

Gauge:

12 dc = 4"

Directions

Ch 5, join with sl st to make a ring.

Rnd 1:   Ch 1, 8 sc into ring, join.

Rnd 2:   Ch 4, *(sl st in next st, ch 3), repeat from * around, join in 1st st of 1st ch sp. (8 ch-3 sps)

Rnd 3:   Ch 1, 1 sc in ch-3 sp, ch 4, *(1 sc in next ch-3 sp, ch 4), repeat from * around, join. (8 ch-4 sps)

Rnd 4: Ch 1, 5 sc in ea ch-4 sp around, join. (40 sts)

Rnd 5: Ch 1, 1 hdc in ea st around, join. (40 sts)

Rnd 6: Ch 1, *(1 dc in next 2 sts, 2 dc in next st), repeat from * around, join. (54 sts)

Rnd 7: Ch 2, 1 dc in ea st around, join.

Rnd 8: Ch 2, *(1 dc in next 8 sts, 2 dc in next st), repeat from * around, join. (60 sts)

Rnd 9: Ch 2, 1 dc in ea st around, join.

Rnd 10: Ch 3, *(sk next st, 1 hdc in next st, ch 1), repeat from * around, join. (29 sts)

Rnd 11: Ch 3, *(1 hdc in next st, ch 1), repeat from * around, join.

Rnd 12: Ch 2, 1 dc in ea st around, join.

Rnd 13: Ch 2, 1 hdc in ea st around, join. Fasten off.

Adding elastic

Using a weaving needle, weave elastic through last rnd and pull it tight enough to fit securely around a bun, but not so tight that you can't put it on. Tie a knot in the elastic and put a tiny bit of glue on the knot.

You want the elastic tight enough to hold your bun but not so snug that you can't get it on. Cover the elastic, following the directions on page 29.

The MC

This is a classic baseball cap. Crocheted in a solid color or with stripes, it's the perfect complement to jeans.

Materials needed:

One 3.5 oz (100 g) skein worsted-weight yarn each in colors A, B, and C. Color A is the main color.

Size G/6 (4 mm) crochet hook for Small, or size needed to obtain gauge

Size H/8 (5 mm) crochet hook for Medium, or size needed to obtain gauge

Size J/10 (6 mm) crochet hook for Large, or size needed to obtain gauge

For making bib, size G/6 (4 mm) crochet hook

For covering elastic, size H/8 (5 mm) crochet hook

Round cord elastic

Weaving needle

Gauge:

With size G hook: 16 sc = 4"

With size H hook: 14 sc = 4"

With size J hook: 13 sc = 4"

Directions

Using color A, ch 4 and join with sl st to form a ring.

Rnd 1:   Ch 1, 10 sc into ring, join.

Rnd 2:   Ch 1, 2 sc in 2nd st from hook, 2 sc in ea st around, join. (20 sts)

Rnd 3:   Ch 1, 1 sc in 2nd st, *(2 sc in next st, 1 sc in next st), repeat from * around, join. (30 sts)

Rnd 4:   Ch 1, 1 sc in 2nd st, 1 sc in next st, *(2 sc in next st, 1 sc in next 2 sts), repeat from * around, join. (40 sts)

The MC... continued

Rnd 5: Ch 1, 1 sc in 2nd st, 1 sc in ea st around, join. (40 sts)

Rnd 6: Ch 1, *(1 sc in next 3 sts, 2 sc in next st), repeat from * around, join. (50 sts)

Rnd 7: Ch 1, *(1 sc in next 4 sts, 2 sc in next st) repeat from * around, join. (60 sts)

Rnds 8–9: Repeat Rnd 5. (60 sts)

Rnd 10: Ch 1, *(1 sc in next 5 sts, 2 sc in next st), repeat from * around, join. (70 sts)

Rnd 11: Ch 1, 1 sc in 2nd st from hook, 1 sc in ea st around, join. (70 sts)

Rnd 12: Ch 1, *(1 sc in next 6 sts, 2 sc in next st), repeat from * around, join. (80 sts)

Rnds 13–15: Repeat Row 11. (80 sts). Cut off yarn. Join color B.

Rnds 16–20: Repeat Row 11. (80 sts). Cut off yarn. Join color C.

Rnds 21–26: Repeat Row 11. (80 sts). Cut off yarn. Join color A

Rnd 27: Repeat Row 11. (80 sts). Do not fasten off.

Adding elastic

With a weaving needle, weave the elastic through the last row, then cover it, following the directions on page 29. Fasten off.

Making the bib

Use size G hook and 2 strands of color A. With the right side of the hat facing, sk the first 25 sts. Join yarn in the 26th st.

Row 1: Ch 1 (count as 1st st now and throughout), 1 sc in next st, *(2 sc in next st, 1 sc in next 2 sts). Repeat from * until 22 sts total.

Row 2: Ch 1, turn, (in back loops only for this row) 1 sc in 2nd st and in each st to end of row, 1 hdc in last row of hat, 1 sl st in next 2 sts. (26 sts)

Row 3: Ch 1, turn, 1 sc in 2nd st and in each st to end of row, 1 hdc in last row of hat, 1 hdc in last row of hat, 1 sl st in next 2 sts. (29 sts)

Row 4: Ch 1, turn, 1 sc in 2nd st, *(1 sc in next 3 sts, 2 sc in next st), repeat from * to end of row, 1 hdc in last row of hat, 1 sl st in next 2 sts. (39 sts)

Row 5: Repeat Row 3. (43 sts) Fasten off.

Queen

This modern B-Girl pattern gives a hip-hop twist to an ancient African design.

Materials needed:

One 3.5 oz (100 g) skein sport-weight cotton yarn

Size I/9 (5.5 mm) crochet hook, or size needed
to obtain gauge

Gauge:

16 dc = 4"

Directions

Ch 24.

Row 1: 1 dc in 3rd ch from hook, 1 dc in ea ch to end. (23 sts)

Row 2: Ch 2 (count as 1st st now and throughout), turn, 1 dc in 2nd st, 1 dc in next 2 sts, *(sk next st, 1 dc in next 4 sts), repeat from* 2 more times, sk next st, 1 dc in last 3 sts. (19 sts)

Row 3: Ch 2, turn, 1 dc in 1st st, 1 dc in ea st until last st from end, 2 dc in last st. (21 sts)

Row 4: Ch 2, turn, 1 dc in 1st st, 1 dc in ea st until last st from end, 2 dc in last st. (23 sts)

Row 5: Ch 2, turn, 1 dc in 1st st, 1 dc in ea st until last st from end, 2 dc in last st. (25 sts)

Row 6: Ch 2, turn, 1 dc in 1st st, 1 dc in ea st until last st from end, 2 dc in last st. (27 sts)

Row 7: Ch 2, turn, 1 dc in 1st st, 1 dc in ea st until last st from end, 2 dc in last st. (29 sts)

Row 8: Ch 2, turn, 1 dc in 1st st, 1 dc in ea st until last st from end, 2 dc in last st. (31 sts)

Rows 9–21: Ch 2, turn, 1 dc in 2nd st, 1 dc in ea st to end. (31 sts)

Row 22: Ch 2, turn, 1 dc in 2nd st, 1 dc in next 19 sts. (21 sts)

Row 23: Ch 2, turn, 1 dc in 2nd st, 1 dc in next 17 sts. (19 sts)

Row 24: Ch 2, turn, 1 dc in 2nd st, 1 dc in next 15 sts. (17 sts)

Row 25: Ch 2, turn, 1 dc in 2nd st, 1 dc in next 13 sts. (15 sts)

Row 26: Ch 2, turn, 1 dc in 2nd st, 1 dc in next 11 sts. (13 sts)

Row 27: Ch 2, turn, 1 dc in 2nd st, 1 dc in next 9 sts. (11 sts)

Row 28: Ch 2, turn, 1 dc in 2nd st, 1 dc in next 7 sts. (9 sts)

Rows 29–32: Ch 2, turn, 1 dc in 2nd st, 1 dc in next 5 sts. (7sts)

Row 33: Ch 2, turn, 1 dc in 2nd st, 1 dc in next 3 sts. (5 sts)

Row 34: Ch 2, turn, 1 dc in 2nd st, 1 dc in next st. (3 sts)

Row 35: Ch 2, turn, 1 dc in 2nd st, ch 1. (2 sts) Work a sc edging around panel.

Repeat for a total of two panels.

Finishing

Join panels with sl st seam (see page 27) around top and shorter side.

Join yarn at one edge and work a sc edging around entire wrap. Fasten off.

Putting on a Queen

Putting on this head wrap is simple.

Get you hair in a bun, then put your wrap on, like you would a hood.

With both hands, grab the ends of the wrap and cross them behind your neck, under your bun, pulling as tight as you would like.

Bring the ends up and cross them.

Pull on the ends until they're tight up against your bun.

Bring the ends down under the bun and tie them. Tuck in any loose ends.

Square Biz

This style is great for kids and teens. Feel free to be creative with your color combos to add flair to this classic crochet design.

Materials needed:

One 3.5 oz (100 g) skein worsted-weight yarn each in colors A, B, C, and D

Size H/8 (5 mm) crochet hook, or size needed to obtain gauge

Weaving needle

Round cord elastic

Gauge:

14 dc = 4"

Size:

4 squares = Small/Medium,
5 squares = Large/X-large

Directions

Using color A, ch 5, join with sl st to form ring.

Rnd 1:   Ch 3 (count as 1st st), 3 dc into ring, ch 3, *(4 dc into ring, ch 3), repeat from * twice, join. (20 sts). Cut off yarn.
Join color B.

Rnd 2:   Ch 3 (count as 1st st), *(sk next 2 sts, 1 dc into next st, [2 dc, ch 3, 2 dc] in next ch-3 sp,** 1 dc into next st); repeat from * twice, then repeat from * to ** one time, join. (24 sts). Cut off yarn.
Join color C.

Rnd 3:   Ch 5 (count as 1st st), *(1 dc in next 3 sts, [2 dc, ch 3, 2 dc] in next ch-3 sp,** 1 dc in next 3 sts, ch 2), repeat from * twice, then repeat from * to ** one time, 1 dc in next 2 sts, join in 3rd st of ch 5. (40 sts). Cut off yarn.
Join color D.

Rnd 4:   Ch 1, *(2 hdc in next ch-2 sp, 1 hdc in next 5 sts, [2 hdc, ch 2, 2 hdc] in next ch-3 sp,** 1 hdc in next 5 sts), repeat from* twice, then repeat from * to ** one time, 1 hdc in last 4 sts, join. (64 hdc). Fasten off.

Repeat to make required number of squares.

Joining squares

Hold 2 squares together with right sides facing. With color C, join using a sl st seam (see page 27). Join remaining squares in same manner, then join first and last squares to create a fabric tube.

Adding elastic

Using a weaving needle, weave in the elastic, then cover it using color C yarn, following the directions on page 29. Fasten off.

Closing the top

Join color C at any seam on the end without elastic.

Rnd 1:   Ch 2, (in back loops only for this round) *(1 dc in next 3 sts, sk next st), repeat from * around, join.

Rnds 2–3:   Ch 2, *(1 dc in next 3 sts, sk next st), repeat from * around, join.

Rnds 4–5:   Ch 2, *(1 dc in next 2 sts, sk next st), repeat from * around, join.

Rnd 6:   Ch 1, *(1 hdc in next st, sk next st), repeat from * around, join.

Join hole with sl st on wrong side.

Talkin' Blues

This hat is one of my clients' favorites. It can be made in so many different color combinations that it is hard to make the same hat twice. The panel seams, which normally would be hidden inside, are actually an exterior detail.

Materials needed:

One 3.5 oz (100 g) skein worsted-weight yarn each in colors A, B, C, and D

Size F/5 (3.75 mm) crochet hook, or size needed to obtain gauge

For making bib, size G/6 (4 mm) crochet hook

For covering elastic, size H/8 (5 mm) crochet hook

Weaving needle

Round cord elastic

Gauge:

16 dc = 4"

Directions

Using color A, ch 10.

Row 1:	1 dc in 2nd ch from hook and in ea ch to end. (9 sts)
Row 2:	Ch 2 (count as 1st st now and throughout), turn, 1 dc in first st, 1 dc in ea st to end. (10 sts)
Row 3:	Repeat Row 2. (11 sts). Cut off yarn. Join color B.
Row 4:	Ch 2, 1 hdc in first st, 1 hdc in ea st to end. (12 sts). Cut off yarn. Join color C.
Row 5:	Ch 2, 1 dc in first st, 1 dc in ea st to end. (13 sts)
Rows 6–7:	Repeat Row 5. (14 sts). Cut off yarn. Join color B.
Row 8:	Repeat Row 4. (16 sts). Fasten off. Join color D.
Row 9:	Repeat Row 5. (17 sts)
Rows 10–11:	Repeat Row 1. (17 sts). Fasten off. Make 5 more panels for a total of 6 panels.

Use single crochet to join the panels.

Joining panels

Use color B to join the panels. Working with 2 panels at a time, with wrong sides facing, match panel rows along edges. Join panels using a sc seam (see page 000), working through both loops. Fasten off. Repeat until all panels are joined, then join first and last panels to form a tube.

Closing the top

Begin closing the top of the hat with a round of half double crochet.

With wrong side facing, join color B at any seam of smaller end of hat.

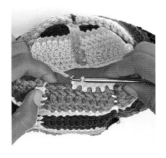

Join color B at a seam for the edging.

Rnd 1: Ch 1, *(1 hdc in next 5 sts, sk next st), repeat from * around, join.

Rnd 2: Ch 2, *(1 dc in next 3 sts, sk next st), repeat from * around, join.

Rnd 3: Ch 2, *(1 dc in next 2 sts, sk next st), repeat from * around, join.

Rnd 4: Ch 2, *(1 dc in next st, sk next st), repeat from * around, join.

Rnd 5: Ch 1, *(1 hdc in next st, sk next st), repeat from * around, join.
Close hole with sl st. Fasten off.

Edging and adding elastic

With right side facing, join color B at any seam on larger end.

Rnd 1: Ch 1, 1 hdc in ea st around, join.

Rnd 2: Ch 1, *(1 hdc in next 5 sts, sk next st), repeat from * to end.

Rnd 3: Repeat Rnd 1. Don't fasten off.

With a weaving needle, weave the elastic through Rnd 3, then cover it using color B, following the directions on page 29.

Making the bib

Use size G hook and 2 strands of color B. Center the bib over three panels as follows: Pick a panel and, with right side facing, find the center stitch of that panel along the edge (each panel is 17 sts wide on its long side, so the center stitch would be the 9th st). Counting that st, count 10 sts to the right (the seam should be counted as 1 st). Join the yarn.

Row 1: Ch 1 (count as 1st st now and throughout), 1 sc in next st, *(2 sc in next st, 1 sc in next 2 sts), repeat from * until there are 22 sts total.

Row 2: Ch 1, turn, (in back loops only in this row) 1 sc in 2nd st and in ea st to end, 1 hdc in last row of hat, 1 sl st in next 2 sts. (26 sts)

Row 3: Ch 1, turn, 1 sc in 2nd st from hook and in ea st to end, 1 hdc in last row of hat, 1 sl st in next 2 sts. (29 sts)

Row 4: Ch 1, turn, 1 sc in 2nd st, *(1 sc in next 3 sts, 2 sc in next st), repeat from * to end, 1 hdc in last row of hat, 1 sl st in next 2 sts. (39 sts)

Row 5: Repeat Row 3. (43 sts). Fasten off.

Jam Pony

I was inspired by my Chickasaw and Blackfoot heritage for this design. These ponytail wraps are funky and fashionable. They can be made as small or as large as you like.

Materials needed:

One 1.3 oz (38.1 g) skein sport-weight acrylic yarn

Size F/5 (3.75mm) crochet hook, or size needed to obtain gauge

Weaving needle

Gauge:

15 dc = 4"

Directions

Ch 21.

Row 1:   1 dc in 2nd ch from hook,
            1 dc in ea ch to end.

Rows   Ch 2 (count as 1st st now and throughout),
2–15:   turn, 1 dc in 2nd st from hook, 1 dc in ea st
            to end. (20 sts)

            Work a sc edging around panel,
            with 3 sc in each corner. Fasten off.

            Repeat to make 2 panels total.

Making the strips

Ch 131.

Row 1:   1 sl st in 2nd ch from hook, 1 sl st in
            ea ch to end. Fasten off.

            Repeat to make 2 strips total.

Adding fringe

You will be adding a single-strand fringe to each st along one side of both panels. Cut each yarn strand 20 inches long. Fold it in half, then use your hook to pull the loop just through the st. Take the loose ends of the strand and pull them through the loop. Pull gently to tighten the knot.

After you have added all the fringes, trim the ends even.

Pull the folded end of the fringe through the stitch.

Putting on Jam Pony

To put on your Jam Pony, take one of the strips, fold it in half, and put within arm's reach. Now take one of the panels and wrap it securely crosswise around your ponytail. Hold it in place with one hand.

With the strip, begin at the top of the panel.

With your other hand, grab the folded strip by the folded end and wrap that folded end around the top of ponytail.

Continue to wrap the strip around the middle and bottom of your ponytail. Make sure the strip is wrapped tight enough so the panel does not fall off.

Continue wrapping snugly around the middle and bottom of the panel.

Tie the ends of the strip together with a knot.

Repeat with the other panel and strip.

Secure the ends with a knot.

Vizor

This visor is great for kids and adults. It can be made with worsted-weight cotton yarn and worn in the spring and summer.

Materials needed:

One 3.5 oz (100 g) skeins worsted-weight yarn each in colors A and B

Size F/5 (3.75 mm) crochet hook, or size needed to obtain gauge

For making bib, size G/6 (4 mm) crochet hook

2 or 4 sets of snaps

Sewing needle

Thread (optional)

Gauge:

17 hdc = 4"

Directions

Using color A, ch 10.

Row 1:	1 hdc in 2nd ch from hook and in ea ch to end. (9 sts)
Rows 2–55:	Ch 1, turn, (in back loops only) 1 hdc in 2nd st from hook and ea st to end. (9 sts)

Finishing

Join color B. Work a sc edging around entire headband, with 2 sc in each corner, join. Fasten off.

Making the bib

Use size G hook and 2 strands of yarn in color A.

With right side facing you, count 32 sts from the right end on a long side of the headband and join yarn in the 33rd st.

Row 1:	Ch 1 (count as first st now and throughout), 1 sc in next st, *(2 sc in next st, 1 sc in next 2 sts), repeat from * until 22 sts total.
Row 2:	Ch 1, turn, (using back loops for this row) 1 sc in 2nd st from hook, 1 sc in ea st to end, 1 hdc in last row of hat, 1 sl st in next 2 sts.

Row 3: Ch 1, turn, 1 sc in 2nd st from hook,
*(1 sc in next 3 sts, 2 sc in next st), repeat
from * to end, 1 hdc in last row of hat,
1 sl st in next 2 sts.

Row 4: Ch 1, turn, 1 sc in 2nd st from hook,
1 sc in ea st to end, 1 hdc in last row of hat,
1 sl st in next 2 sts. Fasten off. Join color B.

Row 5: Repeat Row 4.

Adding the snaps

Wrap the headband around your forehead to determine
where you should put the snaps (usually within Rows 2–6).
Use a sport-weight yarn or thread of a similar color to sew
them on. You can also add 2 more sets of snaps to make
the visor adjustable.

With the bib facing away from you, attach the snap
on the underside (wrong side) of the left flap.

Place the ball portion of the snap at the corners,
right underneath color B.

Secure snaps with thread and a sewing needle.
This next step will determine the fit of the visor.

Center the socket portion of the snap with
the corresponding ball portion. Place socket in
whatever row needed to obtain the fit you desire.

Secure snap with needle and thread.

Sew in your snaps.

**If you want to make your Vizor adjustable,
sew in four sets of snaps.**

Kinky Reggae

This mesh-style hat is perfect for a hot day. It can also be made with cotton or sport-weight acrylic yarn. For a totally different look, add the smaller bib on page 32 to it.

You can use a small Kinky Reggae as a bun holder.

Materials needed:

One 3.5 oz (100 g) skein worsted-weight yarn each in colors A, B, and C

Size J/10 (6 mm) crochet hook, or size needed to obtain gauge

For covering elastic, size H/8 (5 mm) crochet hook

Weaving needle

Round cord elastic

Gauge:

16 hdc = 4"

Directions

Large

Using color A, ch 4 and join with sl st to form a ring.

Rnd 1: Ch 1, 10 hdc in ring, join, cut off yarn. Join color B.

Rnd 2: Ch 1, 2 hdc in 2nd st from hook, 2 hdc in ea st to end, join. (20 sts). Cut off yarn. Join color C.

Rnd 3: Ch 1, *(1 hdc in next st, 2 hdc in next st), repeat from * around, join. (30 sts). Cut off yarn. Join color A.

Rnd 4: Ch 3, *(1 dc in next st, ch 1), repeat from * around, join. (30 sts)

Rnd 5: Ch 4, *(1 dc in next st, ch 2), repeat from * around. (30 sts)

Rnds 6–7: Repeat Rnd 5. Cut off yarn. Join color B.

Rnds 8–11: Repeat Rnd 5. Cut off yarn. Join color C.

Kinky Reggae with a bib

Rnds 12–15:	Repeat Rnd 5.
Rnd 16:	Ch 2, *(1 hdc in next ch-2 sp, 1 hdc in next st), repeat from * around, join. Don't fasten off.

Medium

Follow pattern for Large through Rnd 7. Join color B.

Rnds 8–10:	Repeat Rnd 5. Cut off yarn. Join color C.
Rnds 11–13:	Repeat Rnd 5.
Rnd 14:	Ch 2, *(1 hdc in ch-2 sp, 1 hdc in next st), repeat from * around, join. Don't fasten off.

Small

Follow pattern for Large through Rnd 6. Join color B.

Rnd 7:	Repeat Rnd 5.
Rnd 8:	Ch 4, *(1 dc in next st, ch 1), repeat from * around, join.
Rnd 9:	Repeat Rnd 8. Join color C.
Rnds 10–11:	Repeat Rnd 8
Rnd 12:	Ch 2, *(1 hdc in next ch-2 sp, 1 hdc in next st), repeat from * around, join. Don't fasten off.

Adding elastic

Weave the elastic through the last rnd, then cover it using color C, following the directions on page 29. Fasten off.

Be Easy

Add a pom pom or a bib to jazz up this casual style beanie.

Materials needed:

One 3.5 oz (100 g) skein of worsted-weight yarn each in colors A, B, C, and D

Size I/9 (5.5 mm) crochet hook, or size needed to obtain gauge

For covering elastic, size H/8 (5 mm) crochet hook

Weaving needle

Round cord elastic

2-inch by 5-inch cardboard strip (for pom-pom, optional)

Gauge:

14 dc = 4"

Stitch guide:

1 cl = 2 dc

Directions

With color A, ch 4 and join with sl st to form a ring.

Rnd 1:   Ch 1, 10 hdc into ring, join. (11 sts)

Rnd 2:   Ch 2, 1 cl in ea st around, join. (20 sts).
            Cut off yarn.
            Join color B.

Rnd 3:   Ch 2, *(1 cl in next st, 1 dc in next st),
            repeat from * around, join. (30 sts).
            Cut off yarn.
            Join color C.

Rnd 4:   Ch 2, *(2 dc in next st, 1 dc in next 2 sts),
            repeat from * around, join. (40 sts).
            Cut off yarn.
            Join color D.

Rnd 5:   Ch 2, *(2 dc in next st, 1 dc in next 3 sts),
            repeat from * around, join. (50 sts).
            Cut off yarn.
            Join color A.

Rnd 6:   Ch 2, 1 dc in ea st around, join. (50 sts)

Rnd 7:   Ch 3 (count as 1st st), *(sk next dc, 1 cl in next
            st, ch 1), repeat from * around, 1 dc in last st,
            join. (25 cl). Cut off yarn.
            Join color B.

Rnd 8: Ch 2 (count as 1st dc), 1 dc in next ch-1 sp, *(ch 1, skip next cl, 1 cl in next ch-1 sp), repeat from * around, ch 1, join. (25 cl). Cut off yarn.
Join color C.

Rnd 9: Ch 3 (count as 1st st), repeat from * around, 1 dc in last ch-1 sp, join. (25 cl). Cut off yarn.
Join color D.

Rnd 10: Repeat Rnd 8.
Join color A.

Rnd 11: Ch 2 (count as 1st st), 1 dc in next ch-1 sp, skip next cl, *(1 cl in next ch-1 sp, skip next cl), repeat from * around, 1 dc in last ch-1 sp, join. (25 cl). Cut off yarn.
Join color B.

Rnd 12: Ch 1 (count as 1st st), 1 hdc in ea st around, join. Cut off yarn. (50 sts)
Join color C.

Rnd 13: Repeat Rnd 12.
Join color D.

Rnd 14: Repeat Rnd 12.
Join color A.

Rnd 15: Repeat Rnd 12. Don't fasten off.

Adding elastic

With a weaving needle, weave the elastic through the last rnd, then cover it using Color A, following the directions on page 29. Fasten off.

Making a pom-pom (optional)

Following the directions on page 37, make a large pom-pom by wrapping all four yarn colors around the cardboard strip 100 times. Attach pom-pom to top of hat as directed.

Soon Come

This hat is a favorite of some of my celebrity clients. Add a snap to it, and you've got a traditional newsboy-style cap. This version uses three colors, but one color works just as well.

Materials needed:

One 4 oz (113 g) skein worsted-weight yarn each in colors A, B, and C. Color A is main color.

Size G/6 (4 mm) crochet hook for Small, or size needed to obtain gauge

Size H/8 (5 mm) crochet hook for Medium, or size needed to obtain gauge

Size I/9 (5.5 mm) crochet hook for Large, or size needed to obtain gauge

For making bib, size G/6 (4 mm) crochet hook

Weaving needle

Round cord elastic

1 set of #3 snaps (optional)

Sewing needle

Thread

Gauge:

With size G hook: 12 pff sts = 4"

With size H hook: 10 pff sts = 4"

With size I hook: 8 pff sts = 4"

Directions

Using color A, ch 4, join with sl st to form a ring.

Rnd 1:   Ch 1, 6 sc into ring, join.

Rnd 2:   Ch 1, 2 sc in 2nd st from hook and in ea st around, join. (12 sts)

Rnd 3:   Ch 1, 1 pff st in 2nd st from hook and in ea st around, join. (12 sts). Cut off yarn. Join color B.

Rnd 4:   Ch 1, 2 pff sts in 2nd st from hook and in ea st around, join. (24 sts)

Rnd 5:   Ch 1, *(1 pff st in 2nd st from hook, 2 pff sts in next st), repeat from * around, join. (36 sts)

Rnd 6:   Ch 1, 1 pff st in 2nd st from hook, 1 pff st in next st, *(2 pff sts in next st, 1 pff st in next 2 sts), repeat from * around, sk last st, join. (46 sts). Cut off yarn. Join color A.

Rnd 7:   Ch 1, 1 pff st in 2nd st from hook, 1 pff st in next 2 sts, *(2 pff sts in next st, 1 pff st in next 3 sts), repeat from * around, join. (56 sts). Cut off yarn. Join color B.

Rnd 8: Ch 1, 1 pff st in 2nd st from hook and in ea st to end, join. (56 sts). Cut off yarn. Join color C.

Rnd 9: Ch 1, 1 pff st in 2nd st from hook, 1 pff st in next 4 sts, *(2 pff sts in next st, 1 pff st in next 5 sts), repeat from * around, join. (65 sts)

Rnds 10–13: Ch 1, 1 pff st in 2nd st from hook and in ea st to end, join. (65 sts)

Rnds 14–16: Using 2 strands of yarn for remainder of pattern, repeat Rnd 8. Cut off yarn. Join color A.

Rnd 17: Ch 1, 1 sc in ea st around, join. Cut off yarn. Join color B.

Rnd 18: Repeat Rnd 17. Cut off yarn. Join color C.

Rnds 19–20: Repeat Rnd 17. Don't fasten off.

Adding elastic

With a weaving needle, weave the elastic through the last row, then cover it, using color C, following the directions on page 29. Fasten off.

Making the bib

Using size G hook and 2 strands of color C, join the yarn.

With the right side of the hat facing you, sk first 25 sts and join yarn in the 26th st.

Row 1: Ch 1 (count as 1st st now and throughout). 1 sc in next st, *(2 sc in next st, 1 sc in next 2 sts), repeat from * until you have 22 sts total.

Row 2: Ch 1, turn, (in back loops only for this row) 1 sc in 2nd st from hook, 1 sc in each st to end of row, 1 hdc in last row of hat, 1 sl st in next 2 sts. (26 sts)

Row 3: Ch 1, turn, 1 sc in 2nd st from hook, *(1 sc in next 3 sts, 2 sc in next st), repeat from * to end, 1 hdc in last row of hat, 1 sl st in next 2 sts. (33 sts)

Row 4: Ch 1, turn, 1 sc in 2nd st from hook, 1 sc in each st to end, 1 hdc in last row of hat, 1 sl st in next 2 sts. (36 sts)

Row 5: Ch 1, turn, 1 sc in 2nd st from hook, 1 sc in next 4 sts, *(2 sc in next st, 1 sc in next 5 sts), repeat from * to end, 1 hdc in last row of hat, 1 sl st in next 2 sts. (44 sts)

Row 6: Repeat Row 4. (45 sts). Fasten off.

Adding snaps (optional)

Fold the bib in half across to locate the center and place bottom half of snap in 2nd row from edge. Using a sewing needle and thread, secure it to bib. Secure top half of snap to Rnd 15 of hat.

O.G.

This hat is timeless. Men really love it, but ladies, you can pick your favorite color or use a thick fuzzy yarn to add a feminine touch.

Materials needed:

One 8 oz (225 g) skein worsted-weight yarn

Size F/5 (4 mm) crochet hook, or size needed to obtain gauge

Size H/8 (5 mm) crochet hook for brim and covering elastic

½-inch-thick elastic

Safety pin

Sewing needle

Thread

Gauge:

14 pff sts = 4"

Directions

Ch 6, join with sl st to make ring.

Rnd 1: Ch 1, 10 pff st into ring, join.

Rnd 2: Ch 1, 2 pff sts in ea st around, join. (20 sts)

Rnd 3: Ch 1, *(2 pff sts in next st, 1 pff st in next st), repeat from * around, join. (30 sts)

Rnd 4: Ch 1, *(2 pff sts in next st, 1 pff st in next 2 sts), repeat from * around, join. (40 sts)

Rnd 5: Ch 1, *(2 pff sts in next st, 1 pff st in next 3 sts), repeat from * around, join. (50 sts)

Rnd 6: Ch 1, 1 pff st in ea st around, join. (50 sts)

Rnd 7:   Ch 1, *(2 pff sts in next st, 1 pff st in next 4 sts), repeat from * around, join. (60 sts)

Rnd 8:   Ch 1, *(2 pff sts in next st, 1 pff st in next 5 sts), repeat from * around, join. (70 sts)

Rnds 9–18:   Repeat Rnd 6.

Rnd 19:   Ch 3, 1 tr in ea st around, join. Don't fasten off.

Adding elastic

Fold hat in half to shape it. Pull elastic through last row with safety pin, weaving it through the tr crochet. Don't allow the elastic to gather the hat. Sew elastic ends together with sewing needle and thread.

Cover the elastic following the directions on page 29. When doing this, be sure to keep the yarn loose enough not to bend the elastic. Take your time.

Folding the hat will give it a fedora look.

Pulling it through with a safety pin, weave the elastic in and out of the triple crochet stitches of the last row.

Be sure the hat is comfortable on your head before you sew the ends of the elastic together.

Making the brim

Use 2 strands of yarn and size H hook.
With right side facing:

Rnd 1:   Ch 1, (in back loops only for this rnd) *(1 sc in next 5 sts, 2 sc in next st), repeat from * around, join.

Rnd 2:   Ch 1, *(1 sc in next 6 sts, 2 sc in next st), repeat from * around, join.

Rnds 3–6:   Ch 1, 1 sc in ea st around, join, and fasten off.

Soldier

Based on the popular cadet cap, this casual hat is a must-have for any wardrobe.

Materials needed:

One 4 oz (113 g) skein worsted-weight yarn

Size H/8 (5 mm) crochet hook, or size needed
to obtain gauge

For making bib, size G/6 (4 mm)
crochet hook

Weaving needle

Round cord elastic

Gauge:
16 hdc = 4"

Directions

Using size H hook, ch 15.

Row 1:	1 hdc in 2nd ch from hook, 1 hdc in ea ch to end. (14 sts)
Row 2:	Ch 2 (count as 1st st now and throughout), 1 hdc in ea st to end. (14 sts)
Rows 3–52:	Repeat Row 2. (14 sts). Don't fasten off.

Finishing

Work a sc edging along 2 longer sides of panel.
With right sides facing, join shorter sides with a sl st seam
(see page 29).

Turn right side out. Along one of the long sides, work 1 sc in
ea st around.

Adding elastic

With a weaving needle, weave the elastic through the last row
of edging, then cover it, following the directions on page 29.
Fasten off.

Closing the top

With right side facing, join yarn on end without elastic.

Rnd 1:	(In back loops only for this rnd) 1 sc in v ea st around, join.

Rnd 2:   Ch 2, 1 dc in next 3 sts, *(sk next st, 1 dc in next 4 sts), repeat from * around, join.

Rnds 3–4:   Ch 2, 1 dc in next st, *(sk next dc, 1 dc in next 3 sts), repeat from * around, join.

Rnd 5:   Ch 2, *(sk next st, 1 dc in next st), repeat from * around, join.

Rnd 6:   Ch 1, *(sk next st, 1 sc in next st), repeat from * around, join. With wrong side facing, close hole with sl st. Fasten off.

Making the bib

Using size G hook and 2 strands of yarn, with right side facing, join yarn in last row.

Row 1:   Ch 1 (count as first st now and throughout), 1 sc in next st, *(2 sc in next st, 1 sc in next 2 sts), repeat from * until 22 sts total.

Row 2:   Ch 1, turn, (in back loops only for this row) 1 sc in 2nd st from hook and in ea st to end, 1 hdc in last row of hat, 1 sl st in next 2 sts. (23 sts)

Row 3:   Ch 1, turn, 1 sc in 2nd st from hook, *(1 sc in next 3 sts, 2 sc in next st), repeat from * to end, 1 hdc in last row of hat, 1 sl st in next 2 sts. (31 sts)

Row 4:   Ch 1, turn, 1 sc in 2nd st from hook and in ea st to end, 1 hdc in last row of hat, 1 sl st in next 2 sts. (34 sts)

Row 5:   Repeat Row 4. (37 sts). Fasten off.

Top Rankin

These stripes will make you stand out in a crowd, but feel free to make it your way—in one color, in stripes, the panels in one color, with the top and panel stitching in a second color, with or without a bib.

Materials needed:

One 3.5oz (100 g) skein worsted-weight yarn each in colors A, B, C, D, and E. Color B is the main color.

Size G/6 (4 mm) crochet hook, or size needed to obtain gauge

For covering elastic, size H/8 (5 mm) crochet hook

Weaving needle

Round cord elastic

Gauge:

16 dc = 4"

Directions

Using color A, ch 9.

Row 1: 1 dc in 2nd ch from hook, 1 dc in ea ch to end. (8 sts)

Row 2: Ch 2 (count as 1st dc now and throughout), turn, 1 dc in 1st st, 1 dc in ea st to end. (9 sts). Cut off yarn. Join color B.

Row 3: Ch 2, turn, 1 hdc in 1st st, 1 hdc in ea st to end. (10 sts). Cut off yarn. Join color C.

Row 4: Repeat Row 2. (11 sts)

Row 5: Repeat Row 2. (12 sts). Cut off yarn. Join color B.

Row 6: Repeat Row 3. (13 sts). Cut off yarn. Join color D.

Row 7: Repeat Row 2. (14 sts). Cut off yarn. Join color B.

Row 8: Repeat Row 3. (15 sts). Cut off yarn. Join color E.

Row 9: Repeat Row 2. (16 sts). Fasten off. Make 5 more panels for a total of 6 panels.

Joining panels

Use color B to join the panels. Working with two panels at a time, with wrong sides facing, match panel rows alongside edges. Join panels using a sc seam (see page 27), working through both loops. Fasten off. Repeat until all panels are joined.

Use single crochet to join the panels.

Join color B at a seam to begin the edging.

Edging

Join color B at any seam along larger opening of hat.

Rnd 1:   Ch 1, 1 hdc in ea st around, join.

Rnd 2:   Ch 1, *(1 hdc in next 5 sts, sk next st), repeat from * around, join.

Rnd 3:   Repeat Rnd 1. Cut off yarn. Join color A.

Rnd 4:   Ch 1, 1 sc in ea st around, join. Cut off yarn. Join color C.

Rnd 5:   Repeat Rnd 4. Cut off yarn. Join color D.

Rnd 6:   Repeat Rnd 4. Cut off yarn. Join color E.

Rnd 7:   Repeat Rnd 4. Cut off yarn. Join color B.

Rnds 8–9:   Repeat Rnd 4. Don't fasten off.

Adding elastic

With a weaving needle, weave elastic through last rnd, then cover it using color B, following the directions on page 29.

Closing the top

With wrong side facing, join color B at any seam along the smaller opening of the hat.

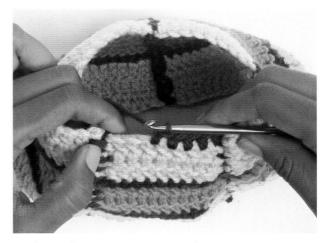

Begin closing the top of the hat with a round of half double crochet.

Rnd 1:	Ch 2, *(1 hdc in next 5 sts, sk next st), repeat from * around, join.
Rnd 2:	Ch 2, * (1 dc in next 3 sts, sk next st), repeat from * around, join.
Rnd 3:	Ch 2, *(1 dc in next 2 sts, sk next st), repeat from * around, join.
Rnd 4:	Ch 1, *(1 hdc in next st, sk next st) repeat from * around, join.
	Close hole with a sl st. Fasten off.

Row 2:	Ch 1, turn, (in back loops only for this row) 1 sc in 2nd st and in ea st to end, 1 hdc in last row of hat, 1 sl st in next 2 sts. (26 sts)
Row 3:	Ch 1, turn, 1 sc in 2nd st from hook and in ea st to end, 1 hdc in last row of hat, 1 sl st in next 2 sts. (29 sts)
Row 4:	Ch 1, turn, 1 sc in 2nd st, *(1 sc in next 3 sts, 2 sc in next st), repeat from * to end, 1 hdc in last row of hat, 1 sl st in next 2 sts. (39 sts)
Row 5:	Repeat Row 3. (43 sts) Fasten off.

After Round 5, close the hole with a slip stitch.

Making the bib (optional)

Use 2 strands of color B. You'll want to center the bib over three panels. Pick a panel and, with the right side facing you, find the center of that panel along the edge (it'll be between the 8th and 9th sts, since each panel is 16 sts wide on its long side). From that point, count 9 sts to the right (count the seam as 1 st). Join the yarn.

Row 1:	Ch 1 (count as 1st st now and throughout), 1 sc in next st, *(2 sc in next st, 1 sc in next 2 sts), repeat from * until there are 22 sts total.

Skully

The skullcap is a basic winter hat. Once you can make your own, be as creative with the colors as you like. I have used what is called variegated yarn in this pattern. I like to work with this type of yarn because you can make a multicolored hat with only one skein of yarn.

Materials needed:

One 4 oz (113 g) skein worsted-weight yarn

Size F/5 (3.75 mm) crochet hook, or size needed to obtain gauge

Gauge:

16 dc = 4"

Directions

Ch 46.

Row 1: 1 dc in 2nd ch from hook, 1 dc in next 38 ch sts, 1 hdc in next 2 ch sts, 1 sc in next 2 ch sts, 1 sl st in last 2 ch sts. (45 sts)

Row 2: Ch 1 (count as 1st st now and throughout), turn, (working in back loops only now and throughout) 1 sl st in 2nd st from hook, 1 sl st in next st, 1 sc in next 2 sts, 1 hdc in next 2 sts, 1 dc in ea st to end. (45 sts)

Row 3: Ch 2, turn, 1 dc in 2nd st from hook, 1 dc in next 38 sts, 1 hdc in next 2 sts, 1 sc in next 2 sts, 1 sl st in last 2 sts. (45 sts)

Row 4 and all even rows through Row 40: Repeat Row 2.

Row 5 and all odd rows through Row 39: Repeat Row 3. Do not fasten off, ch 1.

Skully... continued

Finishing

With wrong side facing, join the first and last rows together using a sl st seam (see page 27). Fasten off.

Closing the top

With right side facing, join yarn at seam.

Rnd 1:   Ch 1, *(1 hdc in next 5 sts, sk next st), repeat from * around, join.

Rnd 2:   Ch 1, *(1 hdc in next 2 sts, sk next st), repeat from * around, join.

With wrong side facing, close hole with sl st. Fasten off.

Lively Up

This design is based on the '80s classic B-Boy "kangol" hat. I've given this version a brim, but you can use a large bib instead (see page 32) or try adding earflaps (see page 34). Have some fun with the color—do the entire brim in a second color, or do the elastic covering and the final row of the brim in a second color.

Materials needed:

Two 3.5 oz (100 g) skeins worsted-weight yarn

Size G/6 (4 mm) crochet hook for Small, or size needed to obtain gauge

Size H/8 (5 mm) crochet hook for Medium, or size needed to obtain gauge

Size I/9 (5.5 mm) crochet hook for Large, or size needed to obtain gauge

For covering elastic, size H/8 (5 mm) crochet hook

Weaving needle

Round cord elastic

Gauge:

With size G hook: 14 dc = 4"

With size H hook: 13 dc = 4"

With size I hook: 12 dc = 4"

Directions

Using 2 strands of yarn, ch 19. Crochet in back loops only throughout.

Row 1:	1 dc in 2nd ch from hook and in ea ch to end. (18 sts)
Row 2:	Ch 2 (counts as 1st st), turn, 1 dc in 2nd st from hook, 1 dc in next 12 sts, 1 hdc in next 2 sts, 1 sc in next 2 sts, 1 sl st in last st. (18 sts)
Row 3:	Ch 1, turn, 1 sl st in 2nd st from hook, 1 sc in next 2 dc, 1 hdc in next 2 hdc, 1 dc in next 13 dc. (18 sts)
Row 4 and all even rows through Row 30:	Repeat Row 2.
Row 5 and all odd rows through Row 31:	Repeat Row 3.

Lively Up with a bib instead of a brim

Finishing

With wrong side facing you, join the first and last rows together using a sl st seam (see page 27).

Work a hdc edging around the wider opening of the hat. Fasten off.

Adding elastic

With a weaving needle, weave the elastic through the edging, then cover it, following the directions on page 29. Fasten off.

Making the brim

Using 2 strands, join yarn at seam on larger end of hat.

Rnd 1: Ch 1, (in back loops only for this rnd) *(1 sc in next 5 sts, 2 sc in next st), repeat from * around, join.

Rnd 2: Ch 1, *(1 sc in next 6 sts, 2 sc in next st), repeat from * around, join.

Rnd 3: Ch 1, *(1 sc in next 7 sts, 2 sc in next st), repeat from * around, join.

Rnds 4–5: Ch 1, 1 sc in ea st around, join. Fasten off.

Closing the top

With wrong side facing and using 2 strands of yarn, join yarn at seam.

Rnd 1: Ch 1, 1 hdc in ea st around, join.

Rnds 2–3: Ch 1, *(sk next st, 1 hdc in next st), repeat from * around, join.

Kool Rock Ski

You'll love the versatility of this hat—you can make the earflaps as long as you'd like and wrap them around your neck like a scarf!

Materials needed:

One 4 oz (113 g) skein worsted-weight yarn each in colors A, B, C, and D. Color B is the main color.

Size I/9 (5.5 mm) crochet hook, or size needed to obtain gauge

For covering elastic, size H/8 (5 mm) crochet hook

Weaving needle

Round cord elastic

2-inch by 5-inch cardboard strip

1-inch by 5-inch cardboard strip (optional)

Gauge:

10 pff sts = 4"

Directions

Using color A, ch 4, join with sl st to form ring.

Rnd 1: Ch 1, 7 pff sts into ring, join. Cut off yarn. Join color B.

Rnd 2: Ch 1, 2 pff sts in 2nd st from hook and in ea st around. (14 sts). Cut off yarn. Join color C.

Rnd 3: Ch 1, 2 pff st in 2nd st from hook, *(1 pff st in next st, 2 pff sts in next st). Repeat from * around, join. (21 sts). Cut off yarn. Join color D.

Rnd 4: Ch 1, 2 pff sts in 2nd st from hook, *(1 pff st in next 2 sts, 2 pff st in next st), repeat from * around, join. (28 sts). Cut off yarn. Join color B.

Rnd 5: Ch 1, 2 pff sts in 2nd st from hook, *(1 pff st in next 3 sts, 2 pff st in next st), repeat from * around, join. (35 sts)

Rnd 6: Ch 1, 2 pff sts in 2nd st from hook, *(1 pff st in next 4 sts, 2 pff sts in next st), repeat from * around, join. (42 sts)

Rnd 7: Ch 1, 2 pff sts in 2nd st from hook, *(1 pff st in next 5 sts, 2 pff st in next st), repeat from * around, join. (49 sts)

Kool Rock Ski with pom-poms on head and earflaps

Kool Rock Ski... continued

Rnd 8: Ch 1, 2 pff sts in 2nd st from hook, *(1 pff st in next 6 sts, 2 pff sts in next st), repeat from * around, join. (56 sts)

Rnds 9–12: Ch 1, 1 pff st in 2nd st from hook, 1 pff st in ea st around, join. Don't fasten off.

Adding elastic

With a weaving needle, weave elastic through last row, then cover it using color B, following the instructions on page 29. Do not fasten off.

Making the earflaps (short version)

Continue with color B.

Row 1: Ch 1, 1 pff st in next 21 sts.

Row 2: Ch 1, turn, 1 pff st in 2nd st, 1 pff st in next 16 sts.

Row 3: Ch 1, turn, 1 pff st in 2nd st, 1 pff st in next 14 sts.

Row 4: Ch 1, turn, 1 pff st in 2nd st, 1 pff st in next 12 sts.

Row 5: Ch 1, turn, 1 pff st in 2nd st, 1 pff st in next 10 sts.

Row 6: Ch 1, turn, 1 pff st in 2nd st, 1 pff st in next 8 sts.

Row 7: Ch 1, turn, 1 pff st in 2nd st, 1 pff st in next 6 sts.

Row 8: Ch 1, turn, 1 pff st in 2nd st, 1 pff st in next 4 sts.

Row 9: Ch 1, turn, 1 pff st in 2nd st, 1 pff st in next 3 sts.

Rows 10–38: Ch 1, turn, 1 pff st in next 2 sts. Fasten off.

To make earflap 2, go back to the beginning of earflap 1. Count over 1 st to the left of 1st row of earflap 1. Join color B and repeat Rows 1–38.

Making the earflaps (long version)

Continue with color B.

Rows 1–9: Repeat Rows 1–9 for short earflaps.

Rows 10–18: Repeat Rows 1–9.

Rows 19–60: Ch 1, turn, 1 pff st in ea st to end. (3 sts) Fasten off.

To make earflap 2, go back to the beginning of earflap 1. Count over 1 st to the left of the 1st row of where you joined yarn for earflap 1. Join color B and repeat Rows 1–60.

Finishing

Begin at back of hat and join color A at 1st st of earflap 1. Work a sc edging around entire hat, including earflaps, with 3 sc in bottom corners of each earflap. Fasten off.

Join color C.

Work 1 sc in ea sc all around, with 3 sc in bottom corners of each earflap. Fasten off.

Join color D.

Work 1 sc in ea sc all around, with 3 sc in bottom corners of each earflap. Fasten off.

Making pom-poms

Following the directions on page 37, make a large pom-pom using the 2-inch-wide cardboard strip and wrapping all yarn colors, held together, around it 100 times. Attach it to the top of the hat as directed. You can also make two small pom-poms to attach to the bottom of each of the earflaps, if you wish. To do this, use the smaller cardboard strip and wrap it 50 times with all of the yarn colors.

Tam

This hat can be worn many ways—make it large and it's perfect for dreadlocks; a small one will fit a child. You can also change the look of it by adding a bib.

Materials needed:

One 4 oz (113 g) skein worsted-weight yarn each in colors A, B, and C. Color C is the main color.

Size G/6 (4 mm) crochet hook for Small, or size needed to obtain gauge

Size H/8 (5 mm) crochet hook for Medium, or size needed to obtain gauge

Size I/9 (5.5 mm) crochet hook for Large, or size needed to obtain gauge

For bib, size G/6 (4 mm) crochet hook

Weaving needle

Round cord elastic

Gauge:

With size G hook: 14 pff sts = 4"

With size H hook: 12 pff sts = 4"

With size I hook: 11 pff sts = 4"

Directions

Using color A, ch 4, join with sl st to form ring.

Rnd 1: Ch 1, 9 pff sts into ring, join. Cut off yarn. Join color B.

Rnd 2: Ch 1, 2 pff sts in ea st around, join. (18 sts). Cut off yarn. Join color C.

Rnd 3: Ch 1, *(2 pff sts in next st, 1 pff st in next st), repeat from * around, join. (27 sts). Cut off yarn. Join color A.

Rnd 4: Ch 1, *(2 pff sts in next st, 1 pff st in next 2 sts), repeat from * around, join. (36 sts)

Rnd 5: Ch 1, *(2 pff sts in next st, 1 pff st in next 3 sts), repeat from * around, join. (45 sts). Cut off yarn. Join color B.

Rnd 6: Ch 1, *(2 pff sts in next st, 1 pff st in next 4 sts), repeat from* around, join. (54 sts)

Rnd 7: Ch 1, 1 pff st in ea st around, join. (54 sts). Cut off yarn. Join color C.

Tam... continued

Rnd 8: Ch 1, *(2 pff sts in next st, 1 pff st in next 5 sts), repeat from* around, join. (63 sts)

Rnd 9: Ch 1, *(2 pff sts in next st, 1 pff st in next 6 sts), repeat from* around, join. (72 sts)

Rnds 10–16: Ch 1, 1 pff st in ea st around, join. (72 sts). Cut off yarn. Join color A.

Rnds 17–18: Ch 1, 1 sc in ea st around, join. (72 sts). Cut off yarn. Join color B.

Rnds 19–20: Repeat Rnd 17. Cut off yarn. Join color C.

Rnd 21: Repeat Rnd 17.

Adding elastic

With a weaving needle, weave the elastic through last rnd, then cover it using color C, following the directions on page 29.

Making a bib (optional)

Using size G hook and 2 strands of color C, sk first 25 sts. Join yarn in 26th st.

Row 1: Ch 1 (count as 1st st now and throughout), 1 sc in next st, *(2 sc in next st, 1 sc in next 2 sts), repeat from * until there are 22 sts total.

Row 2: Ch 1, turn, (in back loops only for this row) 1 sc in 2nd st and in ea st to end, 1 hdc in last row of hat, 1 sl st in next 2 sts. (26 sts)

Row 3: Ch 1, turn, 1 sc in 2nd st from hook and in ea st to end, 1 hdc in last row of hat, 1 sl st in next 2 sts. (29 sts)

Row 4: Ch 1, turn, 1 sc in 2nd st, *(1 sc in next 3 sts, 2 sc in next st), repeat from * to end, 1 hdc in last row of hat, 1 sl st in next 2 sts. (39 sts)

Row 5: Repeat Row 3. (43 sts). Fasten off.

Notty Dread

This style was inspired by the neighborhood of Nostrand and Dean Avenues in Brooklyn, New York. This hat is strictly for the dreads. I always get requests to make hats for people with long locks, because it's hard to find ones that are large enough.

Materials needed:

Color A: One 8 oz (225 g) skein worsted-weight yarn

Color B: One 4 oz (114 g) skein sport-weight yarn

Size H/8 (5 mm) crochet hook, or size needed to obtain gauge

For bib, size G/6 (4 mm) crochet hook

Round cord elastic

Weaving needle

Gauge:

12 dc = 4"

Directions

Using 2 strands of color A, ch 4, join to form a ring.

Rnd 1:	Ch 2 (count as 1st st now and throughout), 11 dc into ring, join. (12 sts)
Rnd 2:	Ch 2, 1 dc into 1st st, 2 dc in ea st around, join. (24 sts)
Rnd 3:	Ch 4, 1 tr in 2nd st from hook, *(ch 1, 1 tr in next st), repeat from * around, join. (24 sts)
Rnd 4:	Ch 2, *(1 dc in ch-1 sp, 1 dc in next st), repeat 3 times, 2 dc in ch-1 sp, 1 dc in next st, repeat from * around, join. (52 sts)
Rnd 5:	Ch 2, *(1 dc in next 4 sts, 2 dc in next st), repeat from * around, join. (62 sts)
Rnd 6:	Ch 1, *(1 hdc in next 4 sts, 2 hdc in next st), repeat from * around, join. (74 sts). Cut off yarn. Join 2 strands of color B.
Rnd 7:	Ch 1, (in the back loops only for this rnd) 1 hdc in ea st around. (74 sts)
Rnds 8–10:	Ch 2, 1 dc in ea st around. (74 sts). Cut off yarn. Join color A.
Rnds 11–12:	Ch 2, 1 hdc in ea st around, join. (74 sts). Cut off yarn. Join color B.

Notty Dread... continued

Rnds 13–14:	Repeat Row 8. Cut off yarn. Join color A.
Rnds 15–16:	Repeat Row 11. Cut off yarn. Join color B.
Rnds 17–18:	Repeat Row 11.
Rnd 19:	Ch 1, 1 sc in ea st around. Fasten off.

Adding elastic

With a weaving needle, weave the elastic through last rnd, then cover it using color A, following the directions on page 29. Don't fasten off.

Making the bib

Use a size G hook and continue with 2 strands of color A.

Row 1:	Ch 1 (count as 1st st now and throughout), 1 sc in next st, *(2 sc in next st, 1 sc in next 2 sts), repeat from * until you have 22 sts total.
Row 2:	Ch 1, turn, (in back loops only for this row) 1 sc in 2nd st from hook, 1 sc in ea st to end of row, 1 hdc in last row of hat, 1 sl st in next 2 sts. (26 sts)
Row 3:	Ch 1, turn, 1 sc in 2nd st from hook, *(1 sc in next 3 sts, 2 sc in next st), repeat from * to end, 1 hdc in last row of hat, 1 sl st in next 2 sts. (33 sts)
Row 4:	Ch 1, turn, 1 sc in 2nd st from hook, 1 sc in ea st to end, 1 hdc in last row of hat, 1 sl st in next 2 sts. (36 sts)
Row 5:	Ch 1, turn, 1 sc in 2nd st from hook, 1 sc in next 4 sts, *(2 sc in next st, 1 sc in next 5 sts), repeat from * to end, 1 hdc in last row of hat, 1 sl st in next 2 sts. (44 sts)
Row 6:	Repeat Row 4. (45 sts). Fasten off.

Superfly

This sleek style hat has a modern look. It goes great with a leather jacket. The directions here are for a solid-color hat, but as you can see from the photos, you can add stripes in contrasting colors or in more subtle tones of the same color.

Materials needed:

Two 8 oz (225 g) skeins worsted-weight yarn
Size H/8 (5 mm) hook, or size needed to obtain gauge
Weaving needle
Round cord elastic

Gauge:

12 hdc = 4"

Directions

Using 2 strands of yarn, ch 5 and join with sl st to form a ring.

Rnd 1:	Ch 1, 10 hdc into ring, join.
Rnd 2:	Ch 1, 2 hdc in ea st around, join. (20 sts)
Rnd 3:	Repeat Row 2. (40 sts)
Rnd 4:	Ch 1, 1 hdc in ea st around. (40 sts)
Rnd 5:	Ch 1, *(2 hdc in next st, 1 dc in next 5 sts), repeat from * around, 1 hdc in last 3 sts, join. (47 sts)
Rnd 6:	Repeat Rnd 4.
Rnd 7:	Ch 1, *(2 hdc in next st, 1 hdc in next 6 sts), repeat from * around, 1 hdc in last 4 sts, join. (54 sts)
Rnd 8:	Ch 1, *(2 hdc in next st, 1 hdc in next 7 sts), repeat from * around, 1 hdc in last 5 sts, join. (61 sts)
Rnds 9–14:	Repeat Rnd 2.
Rnd 15:	Ch 1, *(2 hdc in next st, 1 hdc in next 8 sts), repeat from * around, 1 hdc in last 6 sts, join. (68 sts)
Rnd 16:	Ch 1, *(2 hdc in next st, 1 hdc in next 9 sts), repeat from * around, 1 hdc in last 7 sts, join. (75 sts). Don't fasten off.

Superfly... continued

Adding elastic

With a weaving needle, weave the elastic through the last rnd, then cover it, continuing with 2 strands of yarn and following the directions on page 29. Don't fasten off.

Making the brim

With the right side facing you, continue with 2 strands of yarn.

Rnd 1:   Ch 1, (in back loops only for this rnd), *(1 sc in next 5 sts, 2 sc in next st), repeat from * around, 1 sc in last 4 sts, join.

Rnd 2:   Ch 1, *(1 sc in next 6 sts, 2 sc in next st), repeat from * around, join.

Rnd 3:   Ch 1, *(1 sc in next 7 sts, 2 sc in next st), repeat from * once more, 1 sc in ea remaining st, join.

Rnds 4–8:   Ch 1, 1 sc in ea st around, join.

Rnd 9:   Ch 1, *(1 sc in next 5 sts, 2 sc in next st), repeat from * around, join. Fasten off.

Resources

These are just a few resources that I use on a regular basis. The Internet has a vast array of information and lists of local crochet groups that you can join in your area.

Brands of Yarn

These are some of my favorite yarns because they are inexpensive, wash well, and have a great range of colors.

Bernat®
www.bernat.com

Lion Brand Yarn®
www.lionbrand.com

Patons®
www.patonsyarns.com

Red Heart®
www.herrschners.com

JCA/Reynolds®
35 Scales Ln.
Townshend, MA 01469
978-597-8794

Sugar 'n Cream
www.sugarncream.com

Retailers

Local yarn stores usually have unique yarns that you can't find in the chain stores, but they are usually more expensive. Some of them have sales, and that is the best time to rack up. Check your yellow pages.

In thrift stores you can sometimes find vintage yarn in colors they don't make any more. You probably won't be able to find enough to make an entire project, but they are great to use as accent colors.

Hobby Lobby℠
www.hobbylobby.com

Jo-Ann Fabric & Crafts℠
www.joann.com

Michaels℠
www.michaels.com

Smiley's Yarns
92-06 Jamaica Avene
Woodhaven, NY 11421
Store: 718-849-9873
Mail Order: 718-847-2185
www.smileysyarns.com

Wal-Mart℠
www.walmart.com

Mail-Order and Internet

Herrschners
www.herrschners.com
This mail-order catalog has great prices and a wonderful variety. It's also one of the few places I have seen that sells great colors of cotton yarn by the cone!

www.purplekittyyarns.com
They sell yarn, needles, pattern books, and more.

Yarnmarket
www.yarnmarket.com
They have a great variety of textured and unique yarns.

Index

About the Author

Hailing from St. Paul, Minnesota, Afya Ibomu comes from a family of needlework artists. However, it wasn't until her early 20s that Afya took up the art of crochet. Since that time, her Brooklyn-based custom-order crochet business, Who the Cap Fits, has blossomed among regular folk and celebrities alike. WTCF-crocheted creations have adorned such entertainers as Erykah Badu, Common, Talib Kweli, Dead Prez, Eric Benet, Dwayne Wiggins (of Tony! Toni! Toné!), and Musiq; graced the pages of *Complex* and *JET* magazines; and continue to make "guest appearances" in music videos by some of today's most recognizable rap and soul artists. Afya's handiwork is sold in Brooklyn boutiques and specialty stores along the East Coast and at internationally-known cultural festivals, and she is a much sought-after vendor in the eclectic world of Manhattan flea markets. To get in touch with her, please contact her at www.getyourcrocheton.com.